The Military Chaplain

CLARENCE L. ABERCROMBIE III

Foreword by BRUCE M. RUSSETT

VOLUME 37
SAGE LIBRARY OF
SOCIAL RESEARCH

 SAGE PUBLICATIONS   Beverly Hills   London

Copyright © 1977 by Sage Publications, Inc.

All rights reserved. No part of this book may be reproduced or utilized in any form or by any means, electronic or mechanical, including photocopying, recording, or by any information storage and retrieval system, without permission in writing from the publisher.

For information address:

    SAGE PUBLICATIONS, INC.
    275 South Beverly Drive
    Beverly Hills, California 90212

    SAGE PUBLICATIONS LTD
    St George's House / 44 Hatton Garden
    London EC1N 8ER

Printed in the United States of America

Library of Congress Cataloging in Publication Data

Abercrombie, Clarence L., III
    The military chaplain.

    (Sage library of social research; v. 37)
    Bibliography: p. 183
    1. Chaplains, Military. I. Title.
UH20.A23   355.3'47'01   76-46555
ISBN 0-8039-0669-2
ISBN 0-8039-0670-6 pbk.

FIRST PRINTING

CONTENTS

Chapter		Page
	Foreword by Bruce M. Russett	7
	Preface	11
	Introduction: The Scope and Purpose of the Book	15
1.	Legitimacy and Religion: Partners or Opponents?	21
2.	Pastors to God's Chosen Peoples: A Brief Sketch of Military Chaplains and American Preachers	31
3.	From Sample Selection to Paper-Shredders, or The Hard Mechanics of Researching the Chaplaincy	47
4.	The Claims of Caesar and God: Differentiating the Role Expectations and Values of Civilian Clergymen from Those of Military Commanders	65
5.	"Choose you this day....": Which Roles and Values the Chaplains Actually Affirm	87
6.	Current Views of the Chaplain and His Attitudes: A Brief Sketch of the Literature	101
7.	Chaplains, Too, Are People, or The Nonexplanation of Variance	111
8.	Further Reflections and Conclusion	135
	Appendix	153
	Bibliography	183
	About the Author	191

FOREWORD: THE COIN SOMETIMES BEARS TWO FACES

In this bicentennial summer I am taking part in a small world affairs program in the northwestern part of Connecticut. The next town is named New Canaan. Here is a constant reminder of a theme Clarence Abercrombie develops in this book: Many early American settlers explicitly considered themselves to be a New Israel, God's Chosen People in the new world. As a result, says Abercrombie, one of the most rending tensions addressed by classical political and religious philosophy—the conflicting demands of church and state—never fully developed in the United States. If Americans were part of a Holy Nation, then service to America was also service to God. A military chaplain, marching on to war, could be doing God's work.

In a more secular age, when Americans are more skeptical and more self-deprecatory, such notions seem offensive as well as quaint. Contemporary Americans are less likely to allow such a central role to religion. Americans who go abroad as religious missionaries are far fewer now than a century ago. Even the American secular faith in the redeeming character of democracy, as manifested in what Arthur Schlesinger, Jr., has called the "liberal evangelism" epitomized by Woodrow Wilson, is in disrepute. Many would be satisfied to make the world safe for *this* democracy; hope of converting the authoritarian heathen to the practice of the democratic creed has faded. Perhaps we do live in Canaan. But we wonder which people we really are. Are we already settled in the new land, the Chosen People with their inheritance? Sometimes we seem more like the old Canaanites, about to lose our land of milk and honey before the attack of a new Joshua.

One might imagine that in a secular age any tension between state and conscience would be further diminished. As the church's command over conscience weakens, the state may strengthen its own. But in contemporary America this surely is not true. While institutionalized churches may have lost authority, people do not necessarily lose their independence of conscience. Indeed, many of the same social processes that have fed secular disbelief have fed a delegitimation of traditional patriotism. Some may say, "my country right or wrong," but many are now more prone to judge their country wrong, and to act on that decision. Though often secularized, a sense of ethical imperatives remains. Though Americans' sense of conscience may be fragmented rather than unified by faith, conflicts between conscience and state, if not between church and state, remain. Memories of the rending of American society during the Vietnam War linger as reminders.

Despite the blending of some state and religious authority for those who believed in the New Israel, conscience and state have often conflicted in America, as in the old world. If in the early colonies many citizens thought of themselves as a New Israel, they rarely agreed about which of their tribes possessed God's truth. The American separation of church and state was innovative, delicate, and necessary in a land of many faiths. Direct conflicts between patriotism and religious conscience were hardly unknown. Merely recall this century's flag salute court decisions regarding the Jehovah's Witnesses, or the almost uniquely American provisions for conscientious objection in war. Indeed, the requirements of religious freedom have contributed vitally to evolving the larger American pluralism of belief and practice that undergirds our democracy.

In recent years political theorists and ethicists have taken renewed interest in theories of the just war. These theories came into particular focus during the Vietnam agony, when American participation in the conflict seemed to violate many of the traditional precepts. More recently, fed by worldwide theological interest as exemplified by some of the documents for Vatican II, and in America spilling over from the Vietnam-stimulated concern, attention has begun to zero in on the conditions (if any) whereby nuclear war might be deemed ethically permissible, and on the circumstances under which people might justly exercise a right of revolution. And of course there are special American as well as more widespread traditions of pacifism, for example, the continuing witness of the Society of Friends.

Retention of these old and sometimes ancient traditions, coupled with the declining reverence for state authority, means that the uni-

Foreword [9]

versal conflict between the claims of God and Caesar remains, even among Chosen People. Secular Americans cannot avoid this conflict as long as they continue to believe that there are standards of right and wrong, derived from whatever source, that sometimes form the basis of conscience-driven acts. Sometimes the state must be resisted, and that resistance driven by more than simply material self-interest. We see that conviction across the globe, and it appears in secular states among purely secular men of conscience. Alexander Solzhenitsyn resisted the Soviet state before he knew Christianity; Andrei Sakharov resists it now, though unprompted by traditional religion. Christians and Marxists alike bear witness in Chile, at the risk of torture.

If conscience is not dead, then students of politics and society may not be indifferent to its force in the systems they study. In his book Abercrombie shows the marks of a social scientist, impelled by a twin loyalty to his religious faith and to the armed forces of the United States, who investigates a special manifestation of problems arising at the juncture of religious and secular loyalties. He focuses on the United States Army chaplaincy, in the period during and immediately following the Vietnam War. At home, many churchmen led the fight against the war being conducted by secular authority. What was the situation of those, especially in the battle zone, who explicitly owed fealty both to their religious denominations and to their military commanders? To what degree, and how, did they find conflict between the two loyalties? Were their beliefs more akin to those held by the professional military officers with whom they served, or to those of their civilian counterparts in the ministry and priesthood? What dilemmas, of private conscience or of public witness before their troops, were created, and how were they resolved? Did the peculiar American symbiosis of religious and secular values mitigate the conflict? From observation of these events, what prognoses might be offered for church, army, and state?

Abercrombie executes this inquiry superbly. He knows something about American history, and especially of evolving religious beliefs and their relation to American society and government. He knows traditional political philosophy, and theology. He knows the army firsthand, as an officer who served his country and who retains a deep affection for many aspects of military life. He brings this depth of personal insight and experience to his work as social scientist, in which he conducts a carefully controlled and well-designed piece of survey research, addressed to chaplains from major religious denominations, civilian clergymen chosen to make an appropriate sample, and regular military officers. After probing members of each group about relevant beliefs and actions, he compares them by systematic statistical analysis. In his conclusion he moves from his specific findings to broader questions, both contemporary and timeless, about civil-military relations, the role of force, and the role of faith in society. Abercrombie's focus is primarily on organized religion and some of its potential conflicts with the state, to the point where some readers might be tempted to conclude that his concerns were not of more general interest. But that would be a very mistaken interpretation. He is dealing with questions of a much broader scope, striking directly at key factors in the efficacy and stability of social systems; no student of society, whatever his or her private beliefs, can ignore these matters. Moreover, almost everyone, whether believer, skeptic, or unbeliever, sometimes has to confront these questions as participant rather than as disinterested observer. All of us have "multiple loyalties," to conviction, to family, to other social groups, and to the state. We are blessed, especially in this time and place, in that the conflict of these loyalties does not too often tear too many of us apart. But it can.

Bruce M. Russett

PREFACE

The shady little town of Jackson is one of my happiest childhood places. I never went there in the winter, but that's just as well, for in those days each year divided itself quite neatly into two parts. The "winter" (which began with the opening of Longino Grammar School on the day after Labor Day) was for dull, grinding grade school work. The "summer" (which began each June 5, or the Friday before) was for slow, undirected contemplation. There was a drugstore in Jackson, right on the town square. It had the old-fashioned four-blade ceiling fans (you can still see them in some parts of Saigon), and you could get a ten-cent limeade squeezed by the proprietor from three real limes. In the summer we used to drive into Jackson about once a week, and I'd wait in that old drugstore while mother bought groceries or daddy picked up some special-sized bolts at the hardware store.

There wasn't much to see in Jackson—just the county courthouse and a few old homes—but the steady drone of the fans and the cool smell of the limes in the summer heat provided stimulus enough for dreams. I always focused my thoughts around one of two Jackson structures, the Confederate Memorial and the Methodist Church. In the space of five minutes I could lead a last gallant charge against Grant's left flank at Appomattox and then preach my thundering sermon on racial justice in the new South. And it always seemed too soon (I was either whipping the Yankees or integrating the church) when daddy drove by to pick me up in our '52 Ford.

Times changed. My family managed to turn the '52 Ford into a '61 Cadillac. We started spending our summers in the mountains instead of the central farm country. And integration finally did come to Jackson (brought, damn it, by the Yankee laws), forcing the closure of the old soda fountain. My dreams, nevertheless, remained much the same;

always, with Word or sword, I wreaked vengeance on the enemies of God and homeland.

Despite two years of active duty as an infantry lieutenant and a flirtation with a preacher's license, I never really became a military man or a clergyman, and in that lack of daydream fulfillment lies the major psychological reason for my choice of the subject matter of this book (the immediate, academic reasons are reserved for presentation in the body of the text).

Without my interest in and affection for soldiers and priests (and therefore especially for chaplains, those soldier-priests), this work would never have been begun. However, that interest alone would not have been sufficient to sustain me throughout the actual research; it took a lot of help from a lot of good friends. To begin, I should thank my graduate school advisors and colleagues in the Yale University Political Science Department; here I include first and foremost Professor Bruce M. Russett. He believed in this project from the very first, and, more important, he believed in me even when the project itself was not going at all well. Similarly, Professor Alfred Stepan's ideas added greatly to any originality or freshness of approach this work may possess. Advisors from other departments also contributed significantly to this research; I am especially grateful for the help of the Rev. Professor Donald Ploch (Yale, Department of Sociology), Professor Sydney E. Ahlstrom (Yale, Department of Religious Studies), and the Rev. Professor Jack S. Boozer (Emory University, Department of Religion). For more recent help and support I should thank my colleagues at Wofford College, especially the Rev. Professor Walter Hudgins and Professor Vivian Fisher. Also, my students in a seminar on the American military criticized most constructively various sections of this work.

My parents gave me love and ceaseless encouragement; together they stuffed about 4000 envelopes, and they also stood ever ready to help me financially. (Thus money, though frequently a problem, was never a worry.) My old friend, Dr. Mark Lovern, and his high school classes in Sandy Springs, Georgia, helped address envelopes for all mailings, and the Adamson family of Arrow Press (Hapeville, Georgia) printed the questionnaires at or even below cost. Mrs. Rosalee Robertson of the Yale Summer Language Institute typed more than 70 pages of the rough draft for no charge, and Ms. Nancy Hope coded hundreds of responses for fifty cents an hour. My pastor, the Rev. Dr. W. Thomas Smith, reviewed questionnaires and manuscripts in virtually all stages of preparation; his criticisms have been of the highest value. My secretary

Preface

at Wofford College, Mrs. Martha Mathews, has cranked off more xeroxing than she cares to remember. My friend Dr. Chris Hope (Clemson University, Department of Sociology) has done little bits of everything, from typing to card-punching to envelope-stuffing. Her incisive criticism from the perspective of a sociologist has been a constant help. Most important of all, she worried along with me through those days when I wondered if my questionnaire response rate would reach 5%!

There are numerous other persons whom I should like to thank—especially those hundreds of clergymen, military commanders, and army chaplains who filled out and returned my rather long questionnaires. I am most grateful to them for their help and consideration. This is really their story, and perhaps it should be dedicated to them. Nevertheless, I feel sure they will understand (and approve) when I name instead a group of people who looked after me and helped me through an even more difficult part of my life.

Thus it is with humble pride that I dedicate this research to the men of the second platoon, Bravo Company, 3rd Battalion (Airborne), 187 Infantry, 101st Airborne Division, and especially to Pfc Don Townsend, who was an infantryman, a friend, and a Christian gentleman.

1976
Spartanburg, South Carolina   C.L.A.

INTRODUCTION: THE SCOPE AND PURPOSE OF THE BOOK

"And they send unto him certain of the Pharisees and of the Herodians, to catch him in his words. And when they were come, they say unto him, Master, we know that thou art true, and carest for no man: for thou regardest not the person of men, but teachest the way of God in truth: Is it lawful to give tribute to Caesar, or not?" But he, knowing their hypocrisy, said to them, "Render to Caesar the things that are Caesar's, and to God the things that are God's." And they marvelled at him.

Mark 12:13-17

"Render to Caesar the things that are Caesar's, and to God the things that are God's." Jesus said it all so simply, but determining which things are whose has caused the problem—and occasionally the agony. We remember first the saints and martyrs: Thomas Becket lying in blood within the great cathedral, Dietrich Bonhoeffer dangling from the Nazi noose, Thomas More (isn't he the only political scientist ever canonized?) standing before the axeman. And then we think of the unnamed thousands of Christians who have been forced, in smaller ways, to choose between the demands of God and Caesar. The problem never ceases to fascinate me—especially as it relates to America, a country that within the space of five years made Thomas More a picture-show hero and Daniel Berrigan a convict.

My first attempt to deal academically with the church-state problem was in an article for *Religion in Life*.[1] This was a basically theological attempt to define the limits to state power recognized by two different exponents of Protestant neo-orthodoxy. The difficulty with such an approach, I was to learn, is that most Christians—indeed, most Christian clergymen—base their religious actions on norms other than the writings of a theological elite. To study the problem in greater depth, it would be necessary to employ the empirical methods of social research.

Although modern political philosophers have often neglected the whole field of religion, the question of religion's relationship to the social order has occupied the minds of many classical thinkers. Machiavelli, for example, hoped that the prince would use religion to provide sacred support for the execution of his policies. Similarly, Karl Marx felt that religion served to legitimate the sociopolitical order that enslaved the proletarian classes. Thomas Hobbes, on the other hand, held that whereas religion might be used to legitimate the policies of the sovereign, it might also provide a rally-point on which men could focus their loyalty—in opposition to the sovereign's absolute authority. Later writers (Durkheim, Pareto, Weber, et al.) continued to debate the question that Hobbes so squarely posed: Does religion tend more to support or, to limit the power of the state? The quest for answers, however, has not been supported by any great amount of empirical investigation, and I hope that my research will provide a useful first step in that direction.

Stated most briefly, I am interested in the relationship of Christianity[2] with the American military. More specifically, I center my investigation around the U.S. Army chaplain: does he act chiefly to legitimate the goals and missions of the military, or does he proclaim a prophetic message that (as it were) cuts vertically across the demands of the military environment—sometimes supporting, sometimes attacking, always transcending? To understand why the chaplaincy is indeed a fit arena for such a study, the reader should gain a sense of what a chaplain is for two institutions most directly concerned with his organizational position: the church and the army. The civilian denominations chosen for this study are basically agreed on what a chaplain should be. He is to be a servant of God to people (who happen to be in uniform), according to the doctrine and tradition of the denomination that has effected his ordination.[3]

For the army, the matter begins almost as simply. The requirements for appointment as a chaplain are quite straightforward; one is eligible for appointment if he is:

1. A male citizen of the United States or one who lawfully entered the United States for permanent residence.
2. Under 33 years of age at the time of actual appointment.
3. Physically qualified.
4. In possession of 120 semester-hour credits of undergraduate study at an accredited college or university and a minimum of 90 semester-hour credits of study performed in an accredited theological school.
5. A regularly ordained clergyman endorsed for the Chaplaincy by a recognized religious denomination.
6. Actively engaged in the ministry as [his] principal vocation in life.
7. Able to receive a favorable National Agency Check.[4]

Introduction: The Scope and Purpose of the Book   [17]

A chaplain is commissioned as a first lieutenant and becomes a captain on his first day of active duty. He can be promoted within the army rank structure up to the rank of brigadier general (Deputy Chief of Chaplains) and major general (Chief of Chaplains). A chaplain can be retained on active duty only as long as he has the endorsement of his parent denomination. He may hold his commission in either the United States Army Reserve, the National Guard of the United States, or the Regular Army. He is subject to the Uniform Code of Military Justice, to the applicable portions of the *Manual for Courts-Martial,* and to all pertinent military regulations. As is the case with medical officers, his rank does not generally carry with it the authority to command troops. The army describes his duties as "analogous to those performed by clergymen in civilian life."[5] Thus it may appear that the army definition of chaplains is the same one used by the civilian denominations—with a lot of military jargon thrown in. Indeed, this is in many ways the case. There is, however, a subtle yet important difference, a difference that leaves open the possibility of conflict.

The First Amendment to the Constitution quite plainly forbids Congress to make any law "respecting an establishment of religion . . . ," and the constitutionality of the military chaplaincy has occasionally been challenged on those very grounds. After all, the Congress authorizes funds that pay the chaplain a salary, transport him with the troops, and provide him chapels in which to preach. It is therefore to be expected that certain parties might wish to challenge the constitutionality of the Chaplain Corps. Thus far, however, the courts have rejected all such challenges, and within the arguments of the chaplaincy's defenders we can see the basic difference between the church's and the army's view of a chaplain.[6]

Briefly, the most cogent defense of the constitutionality of the chaplaincy runs as follows. The commander of a military unit has the final responsibility for the welfare of the men in his unit. Such welfare obviously consists of food, shelter, and the other things that are necessary to support physical life. In another sense, however, human beings have developed welfare needs that go beyond the physical necessities of life. One such "need" (at least for quite a number of people) may be religion. Thus the commander also has responsibility for the religious life of the men in his unit.[7]

Since the commander himself obviously lacks the training to understand personally the religious needs of all his men, the chaplain is appointed as a staff specialist to assist the commander in this phase of his responsibility.[8] Thus the army is not paying (unconstitutionally) a man to perform religious activities; it is instead purchasing the services of a specialist who (*by* performing religious activities) aids unit commanders in fulfilling their responsibilities in securing the welfare of their men.

In other words, the military need not be interested in a chaplain's loyalty to his perception of God's commandments as long as he performs his assigned functions (and, indeed, the authorization of a Chaplain Corps need not imply any official opinion about even God's existence). For the church, on the other hand, the obedience of its minister (including chaplains) to the living will of God is more to be desired than the simple fulfillment of a few formal religious duties. As this research report continues, the reader will see how such a slight difference in interpretation can lead to real tension between the institutional demands of a prophetic church and of the army.

A great deal of the existing literature tends to view the chaplaincy as a role in isolation. This is, I believe, a most serious fault. The chaplain is both an ordained clergyman and a commissioned officer. One cannot expect to understand him apart from either the broader fellowship of his (basically civilian) denomination or the community of his military organization. Therefore I have investigated by mailed questionnaire the attitudes of chaplains, civilian clergymen, and military commanding officers. With respect to certain roles and values, the two latter professions may be said to form a broad continuum along which a chaplain could determine his proper place. In the body of this book I address three closely related questions:

1. In the context of American society, what roles and values are really viewed differently by civilian clergymen and military commanders?
2. With respect to roles and values that are viewed quite differently, where along a military officer-civilian clergyman continuum are chaplains generally located?
3. Are there any factors of military or religious background that will enable us to predict where along the continuum a particular chaplain will be found?

In my attempt to deal systematically with these three questions, I have divided the body of this work into eight chapters.

In the first chapter I develop my working definition of *legitimacy*. Then I briefly discuss various political philosophers' views on the use of

Introduction: The Scope and Purpose of the Book [19]

religion in legitimation. These philosophers stress religion's utility in legitimating a political system, but most also recognize the possibility of religious opposition.

After outlining the history of military chaplains from the earliest biblical references, I turn in Chapter 2 to a historical examination of religion in American society. I suggest that American Christianity has become an arena in which the opposing stresses of church and state (discussed in Chapter 1) can be at least partially resolved. The goals of the American nation have seemed (or perhaps have been) so very "Christian" that American churchmen have seldom perceived even the possibility of a conflict between Caesar and God. The historical rightness of America's causes has appeared to obviate the Christian necessity for a prophetic criticism of government.

In Chapter 3 a description of the selection of my sample and the design of my research instrument is followed by a discussion of my return rates and an attempt to tackle the problem of return bias.

Chapter 4 addresses particularly the first question I raised earlier: What roles and values are really viewed differently by civilian clergymen and military commanders? I rely chiefly on my questionnaire returns, of course, but I also examine certain published expressions of military and religious doctrine.

Chapter 5 attempts to answer question 2: With respect to those roles and values which are viewed quite differently, where along a military officer-civilian clergyman continuum are chaplains generally located? Here again, most of the discussion is taken from my analysis of returned questionnaires.

While the first two major research questions examine the chaplaincy in a context defined by two related professions, the third question focuses on the chaplain per se: What factors in his religious-military background are related to the ways in which he defines his vocation of military priest? Here many of the published writings on the chaplaincy are of relevance. In discussing those works in Chapter 6, I point out where some of their basic assumptions are called into question by the findings of Chapters 4 and 5. I also draw on these works (together with writings on attitude change) to develop certain hypotheses that appear to be relevant to the study of chaplains per se.

Chapter 7 attacks directly my third research question: Are there any factors in a chaplain's military or religious background that will enable us to predict where along the continuum a particular chaplain will be found? Here we note that most of the hypotheses developed in Chapter 6 clearly lack significant explanatory power, and we consider why that is the case.

In the final chapter I attempt to move beyond the rigorous confines of my data; to suggest some possibilities of reform within the chaplaincy. I also point out certain benefits that might accrue to the army and to the nation as a whole if these reforms were to be implemented.

NOTES

1. Clarence L. Abercrombie, III, "Bases in Modern Protestant Theology for a Doctrine of Resistance to the Unjust State: Barth and Bonhoeffer."
2. In this book, Christianity is represented by four major denominations: Lutherans, Roman Catholics, Southern Baptists, and United Methodists.
3. See, for example, "What in the World Is a Chaplain?" by the Division of Interpretation, Program Council of the United Methodist Church; the definitions of the chaplaincy included in this pamphlet are substantially representative of the views held by virtually all the civilian denominations. The denominations recognize, of course, that the opportunities and problems faced by a chaplain differ from those faced by the civilian clergyman, and therefore the methods of the two types of minister may also differ. Nevertheless, all the denominations insist that the chaplain and the civilian clergyman are both involved in what is essentially one ministry.
4. U.S. Department of the Army Pamphlet 165-2, "The Challenge of the Chaplaincy in the United States Army." Pages are not numbered. Since this writing, women too have become eligible for service as chaplains.
5. Ibid.
6. For a more complete discussion of constitutional issues raised by the military chaplaincy, see A. Ray Appelquist (Ed.), *Church, State and Chaplaincy*. It should be noted that federal cours have generally refused to hear challenges to the constitutionality of the chaplaincy.
7. See Army Regulation 165-20. Until the spring of 1973, all cadets and midshipmen (regardless of their religious beliefs, or lack of them) at the service academies were required to attend Sunday chapel. This requirement was justified by the claim that future career officers needed to know about chapel programs in order to fulfill their function of providing for the welfare of their men. The court's recent rejection of this claim may have weakened the constitutional status of the chaplaincy as a whole, and I would not be at all surprised to see the chaplaincy formally challenged in the near future.
8. U.S. Department of the Army Field Manual 16-5, *The Chaplain*, p. 1.

Chapter 1

LEGITIMACY AND RELIGION:

PARTNERS OR OPPONENTS?

Slaves of God, men must also be slaves of Church and State.
Michael Bakunin

The principle that "God must be obeyed more than man" . . . has been the most ancient check on all political power.
Max Weber

Religion appears in history both as a world-maintaining and as a world-shaking force.
Peter L. Berger

It is my impression that virtually all contemporary political theorists discuss the concept of sociopolitical legitimacy—in passing. Their basic models are generally the same: A political system receives information (demands input) from a circle of political actors; the information is processed, and from the system there emanates a set of responses (products output). A system whose products output fulfill (or have in the past fulfilled) to a certain extent the demands input achieves a degree of "legitimacy." Having posited their model, the political theorists decry its inadequacies and demand correctives: The extent of the political-actor circle must be more adequately defined. (What about persons who are subject to the rule of the system and have their input channels blocked?) One must consider the system that acts to *create* demands it can supply easily and to its own benefit. (Are Americans socialized to believe that happiness comes from consuming products that a capitalistic system must produce to survive?) The model must be altered to show that a major system output can be coercive force that demands inputs of services and obedience, which are given of necessity. (Can a viable political society rest mainly on coercive force?) The list of necessary model modifications will grow for a while. Then, having paid their tributes to the concept of legitimacy, the contemporary political theorists proceed to the subjects that constitute their principal concerns.

My criticism is, of course, exaggerated, almost to the point of caricature; yet there is a sense in which it is just: Among the contemporary theorists, sociopolitical legitimacy is a concept more often mentioned than seriously discussed.[1] Furthermore, discussions that do arise are usually centered around an input-output analysis such as I have so cursorily sketched. However, the term "legitimacy" can be used in a much broader context.

The basic meaning of *legitimacy* is "the quality of being according to law." As a child is said to be legitimate if his parents are legally married, so, in this sense, a government is legitimate if it is constituted according to some law or set of laws. Thus in the infancy of the modern nation-state, "legitimacy" was quite properly used in describing the status of the sovereign. The king was said to be the legitimate ruler if he had come to the throne according to the established rules of succession (note the relationship between *legitimacy* in reference to government and *legitimacy* in reference to progeny). Yet the meaning of *law* itself generally extended beyond any particular set of rules established by sovereigns or legislatures; there was a sense in which the laws regulating a political system's functioning were supposed to be in conformity with the natural law ordained by God for the governance of his creation. During the seventeenth and eighteenth centuries such conformity was increasingly seen as a condition for political legitimacy:

> I will not dispute now whether princes are exempt from the laws of their country, but this I am sure: they owe subjection to the laws of God and Nature. Nobody, no power, can exempt them from the obligations of that external law.[2]

* * *

> Whosoever in authority exceeds the power given him by the law, and makes use of the force he has under his command to compass that upon the subject which the law allows not, *ceases in that to be a magistrate* and, acting without authority, may be opposed as any other man who by force invades the right of another.[3]

Thus political legitimacy has come to mean the "rightness" of a political system's holding the place and power it possesses. Often this definition is understood operationally in terms of a system's responsiveness to demands input, but clearly this usage deals with only one type of legitimacy.[4] It is also possible for a political system to be perceived as legitimate because its subjects or citizens believe that the system—beyond its immediate ability to fulfill their demands—is somehow good, right, proper in a *wertrational* sense.[5] Furthermore, it is also possible for a government to be perceived as legitimate simply because it exists, because it holds an important, well-defined place in its citizens' cognitive universe: "In other words, the socially constructed world legitimates itself by virtue of its facticity."[6]

It is chiefly with the latter varieties of legitimacy that my present research is concerned. And a further definitive qualification must also be added at this point: Whenever I refer to the legitimacy of a political system, a government, or a regime, I am using the term in a value-neutral sense. That is, the sentence "Religion legitimates the political system," would *not* mean that religion somehow makes the system objectively good. Rather I should wish it to be understood that religion causes (some or all of) the system's political actors to believe that the system is right or necessary or proper.

The relation of religion to "legitimacy" (though that precise term is seldom used) has fascinated political philosophers since the middle ages. Machiavelli, for instance, insisted that the prince (who rules by power) should encourage the development of any religion that provided sacred support for his office. Such a supportive religious ideology would increase the people's loyalty toward their ruler; it would serve as a nonviolent social control mechanism; thus it would enable the prince to conserve those resources of naked force which are the backbone of his political power.

For Thomas Hobbes the case was more ambiguous. Like Machiavelli, though for different reasons, he was determined to set up an absolute ruler, and he was well aware of religion's potentially supportive role. But he was unable to forget the bloody trauma of England's civil war—a rebellion initiated by issues that were, to a great extent, religious. Hobbes was thus convinced that any belief system making ultimate claims on a people's loyalty could impinge on the authority of the sovereign and eventually disrupt the domestic peace. Such a crisis could develop in either of two ways. First, the commands of the sovereign might conflict with the dictates of an established religion.[7] Hobbes wished to make sure that this did not occur. Therefore he stated that although the sovereign should make no law that conflicted with scripture,[8] the sovereign himself must always have the sole power to define what *is* holy scripture: "Seeing therefore I have already proved, that Sovereigns in their own Dominions are the sole Legislators; those books only are Canonicall, that is, Law, in every nation, which are established by Sovereign authority."[9]

But even if Hobbes' sovereign had absolute control over what was to be called canonical scripture, there remained another way in which religion could work to undermine his legitimacy. According to a major branch of medieval theology,[10] the Bible describes only the usual ways in which God's power manifests itself (the *potentia Dei ordinata*), but God himself, being limitless and omnipotent, can act in ways that transcend those recorded manifestations (he can act according to the *potentia Dei absoluta*). To cement their hold on the people, earthly sovereigns (and often the church as well) take control of the Bible, twist it to fit their political purposes, and claim such texts to be the final word of God. As Thomas Müntzer, ecclesiastical and social revolutionary, said, "The difficulty lies in the fact that the people have been indoctrinated by their clergy to believe that God has already spoken once and for all."[11]

But such claims, according to the theologians, were attempts to deny the *potentia Dei absoluta*. In each fallen person, they held, there remains something of God's image; it is never fully hidden from God's presence, and through this anthropological (rather than institutional) structure, God can come into mystical contact with his people.[12] Christ is thus brought out of history into the present, where he can speak to his followers and lead them wherever he wishes, even in an attack against the state that tries to defy his living will.[13] Thus it is no wonder that the greatest social revolutionaries of the sixteenth and seventeenth centuries (from Müntzer to the Diggers) were basically religious mystics. No wonder that Hobbes was quick to distrust anyone who made a claim to personal revelation!

> It hath been also commonly taught, *That Faith and Sanctity, are not to be attained by Study and Reason, but by Supernatural Inspiration or Infusion,* which granted, I see not why any man should render a reason of his Faith; or why every Christian should not also be a Prophet; or why any man should take the Law of his Country, rather than his own Inspiration, for the rule of his action. And thus we fall again into the fault of taking upon us to Judge of Good and Evil; or to make Judges of it, such men as pretend to be supernaturally inspired, to the Dissolution of all Civil Government.[14]

* * *

If men were at liberty, to take for God's Commandements, their own dreams, and fancies, or the dreams and fancies of private men; scarce two men would agree upon what is God's Commandement; and yet in respect of them, every man would despise the Commandements of the Common-wealth.[15]

* * *

If he [the sovereign] gave away the government of Doctrine, men will be frightened into rebellion with feare of Spirits.[16]

Therefore, "there is no place in the world where men are permitted to pretend other Commandements of God, than are declared as such by the Commonwealth."[17]

Hobbes, then, believed that a commonwealth could profit from religious legitimation. He also saw that to enjoy the fruits of such legitimation without taking any chances on the potentially disruptive effects of religion, the sovereign would have to assume total charge over religious doctrine. Jean-Jacques Rousseau, for his part, believed there had been in pre-Christian nations an identity of state and religion (with the political leaders, if anyone could be differentiated as such, in overall control) so that "each state, having its peculiar form of worship as well as its own government, did not distinguish its gods from its laws."[18] Christianity, however, was different:

Jesus came to establish on earth a spiritual kingdom, which separating the religious from the political system, destroyed the unity of the State, and caused the intestine divisions which have never ceased to agitate Christian Nations.

... a perpetual conflict of jurisdiction has resulted from this double power, which has rendered any good polity impossible in Christian States; and no one has ever succeeded in understanding whether he was bound to obey the ruler or the priest.[19]

Rousseau was quick to pay homage to Hobbes for his attempt to bring Christianity under the sway of civil government:

Of all Christian authors, the philosopher Hobbes is the only one who has clearly seen the evil and its remedy, and who has dared to propose a reunion of the heads of the eagle and the complete restoration of political unity, without which no state or government will ever be well constituted. But he ought to have seen that the domineering spirit of Christianity was incompatible with his system, and that the interest of the priest would always be stronger than that of the State.[20]

In the end, we realize that Rousseau believed strongly in the utility of religious legitimation; he simply did not think Christianity was the religion to provide it.[21]

More recent political philosophers were to revise the assessment of Rousseau. In the nineteenth century, and particularly in the wake of Feuerbach's critiques of Christianity,[22] increasing attention was paid to the role of religion in the state. For the political theorists, society came first, and from within the social context religion was developed to fulfill certain societal needs. Foremost among those proponents of "functional" theories of religion was Karl Marx. He felt that man invented religion as an instinctive protest against his wretched existence; when man said "There must be a God in heaven," he was really stating that "There must be a better life than the one I'm living here on earth." As man began to believe ever more firmly in his religious fantasies, as he placed his hopes on heaven, his world became split into two spheres: Man became alienated.[23] As long as man was in large part alienated from the real world of his material surroundings (as long as he placed his trust on a redemption beyond the real world), he could make no progress in changing the social conditions that gave rise to religious illusions in the first place.

For Marx, then, religion did not offer a direct consecration of the state; rather it supplied a rationale to make acceptable those sufferings the state causes. Such a theology of legitimation was developed primarily to suit the interests of ruling classes. In the Middle Ages, the religious concept of an organic society, with each person fulfilling a particular, God-ordained life role, kept the serfs (and, for a time, the rising bourgeoisie) in their places and enabled the feudal nobility to stay securely on top. Upon coming to power, the bourgeoisie promulgated a religion that consecrated earthly suffering. Thereby duped, Marx wrote, the lower classes initially fail to revolt against the capitalistic system that causes the (consecrated) suffering. After their rise for power (and as they thereby conquer their alienation), the proletariat will recognize the conservative nature of the religious consecration. They will overthrow modern Christianity, even as the bourgeoisie overthrew organic medieval Christendom in the Reformation. Thus the criticism of religion is, at its roots, the criticism of exploitive class rule:

> The abolition of religion as the *illusory* happiness of the people is required for their *real* happiness. The demand to give up the

illusions about its condition is the *demand to give up a condition which needs illusions.* The criticism of religion is therefore *in embryo the criticism of the vale of woe,* the halo of which is religion.[24]

The essential Marxian ideas on religion were shared by Michael Bakunin, who presented them in stronger rhetorical, if less theoretical terms in his pamphlet, *God and the State:*

> Reduced, intellectually and morally as well as materially, to the minimum of human existence, confined in their lives like a prisoner in his prison, without horizon, without outlet, without even a future if we believe the economists, the people would have the singularly narrow souls and blunted instincts of the bourgeoisie if they did not feel a desire to escape; but of escape there are but three methods—two chimerical and a third real. The first two are the dramshop and the church, debauchery of the body or debauchery of the mind; the third is social revolution.[25]

Two other social analysts with functional views of religion were Emil Durkheim and Vilfredo Pareto. Like Marx, both held that religion was produced by society to fill a systems-maintenance function. Durkheim, again like Marx, foresaw the approaching end of religion. Yet far from celebrating the liberation of man that would come with the death of God, he feared the demise of all social and moral order. Durkheim, in fact, hoped to use his new science of sociology to invent a fresh moral belief system that could fill the social ordering role soon to be vacated by religion.[26]

Pareto's analysis was essentially the same as Durkheim's, though he was apparently undisturbed over the imminent collapse of religion. Durkheim viewed with alarm; Marx pointed with pride. Pareto, paradigm of value free social science, displayed only indifference.

Thus the functionalist approach was very popular around the turn of the century. And yet it was incomplete, for even granting that all religious forms are the product of some society, it is historically incorrect to argue that each type of society has in it only the homegrown religious forms of its own production. For example, there is, as Hobbes realized, a sense in which English Christianity is more than simply a product of English society, constructed to support an existing English order. There remains in English Christianity an ethical-religious-philosophical content that did not arise solely from the material conditions of the British Isles and indeed has made its own contribution to the development of English life styles.

Historically, religion has been not only a functional device fabricated by society; it has also been an independent variable capable of acting on the society that surrounds it. The greatest exponent of this view was, of course, Max Weber. In contrast to Marx, he argued throughout *The Protestant Ethic* that Calvinism was *not produced by* a bourgeois class newly come to power; rather, Calvinism *produced* the psychological conditions that enabled capitalism to develop. Although Weber did not entirely neglect the effects of society on religion, he nevertheless emphasized religion as the independent variable.[27] It has thus remained for other, more recent analysts to stress the duality of religion's interactions with society. Peter Berger, for instance,[28] emphasizes a relationship in which society forms religion, but religion also acts to change society, and the changed society, in turn, exerts new effects on religion. One chief effect of religion is to legitimate society by adding metaphysical credence to social definitions of reality:

> Religion has been the historically most widespread and effective instrumentality of legitimation—all legitimation maintains socially defined reality. Religion legitimates so effectively because it relates the precarious reality constructions of empirical societies with ultimate reality.[29]

And yet though religion is able to support much of socially defined reality, there can come a point at which "the precarious reality constrictions of empirial societies" differ so greatly from what a religion defines as "ultimate reality" that the two cannot be reconciled.[30] Then a religion that often supports the society's reality definitions will witness to their untruth.[31] Precisely this situation arose in Nazi Germany. The myths of Aryan spiritual superiority were so obviously opposed to the Christian gospel that a large segment of the German theological elite felt the necessity of rebellion.[32] As Berger said, "religion appears in history both as a world-maintaining and as a world-shaking force."[33] Müntzer and Bonhoeffer and Hobbes would say Amen.

NOTES

1. The discussion by David Easton is better than most; also, he well recognizes the poverty of the existing literature. See Easton, *A Systems Analysis of*

Legitimacy and Religion: Partners or Opponents? [29]

Political Life, p. 279. The classic discussions of Max Weber also deserve more intensive study than many recent theorists appear willing to grant. Weber is most anxious to stress that input-output models usually neglect the importance of such intangible factors as charisma in building legitimacy. The recent translation (1968) of Weber's massive *Economy and Society* may provide impetus for the necessary study. (And incidentally, the discussion of types of legitimate authority that appears in *Economy and Society* should answer at least some of Easton's criticisms of Weber's ideas on legitimacy.)

2. John Locke, *The Second Treatise on Government,* p. 109.
3. Ibid., p. 114, emphasis supplied.
4. Weber would call this a form of legal-rational legitimacy; see his *Economy and Society,* p. 215 or *Charisma,* pp. 12, 46.
5. See Weber, *Charisma,* pp. 11-12.
6. Peter L. Berger, *The Sacred Canopy,* p. 30. Consider also premodern China's mandate-of-heaven concept of legitimacy: The bare fact that a government exists, performing the ritual acts, is prima facie evidence of that government's moral legitimacy.
7. For Hobbes, of course, the only religion to be seriously considered was Christianity.
8. The extent to which Hobbes himself believed this is open to question. Perhaps the religious climate of the sixteenth century made it prudent to include such a defense (albeit lukewarm) of religion's primacy; after all, Hobbes did not wish to be known as an atheist.
9. Thomas Hobbes, *Leviathan,* Ch. 33, p. 415.
10. This train of theological thought, though strong in Protestantism, was to cut across the sectarian dichotomy that developed during the Reformation.
11. Steven E. Ozment, *Mysticism and Dissent,* p. 19.
12. Ibid., pp. 30, 51, 55.
13. Ibid., pp. 90-91, 105.
14. Hobbes, Ch. 29, p. 366, emphasis Hobbes'.
15. Ibid., Ch. 26, p. 333.
16. Ibid., Ch. 18, p. 236.
17. Ibid., Ch. 26, pp. 333-334.
18. Jean-Jacques Rousseau, *The Social Contract,* p. 137.
19. Ibid., pp. 138-139.
20. Ibid., p. 140.
21. Ibid., pp. 140-147.
22. Like Rousseau, Ludwig Feuerbach believed that Christianity did entail a split between social and religious realms. Man projected his wants and needs—projected the sort of being he essentially wanted to be—on his (imaginary) gods. God thus became an expression of man's alienation from his essential self. See *The Essence of Christianity.*
23. Shlomo Avineri, *The Social and Political Thought of Karl Marx,* p. 18. Note the influence of Feuerbach.
24. From Karl Marx's "Contribution to the Critique of Hegel's Philosophy of Right," found in Marx and Friedrich Engels, *On Religion,* p. 42. The emphasis is Marx's.
25. Michael Bakunin, *God and the State,* p. 16. Bakunin believed that non-

religious (even Marxist) ideology could also legitimate suffering. Ibid., pp. 40-41, 47, 55.

26. Emil Durkheim, *Suicide,* see especially Ch. 3 of Book 3.

27. Perhaps this was because he consciously tried to provide a corrective to Marx's strictly materialistic-functional approach.

28. See especially *The Sacred Canopy.*

29. Ibid., p. 32.

30. Within the mainstreams of Christian theology, such a situation may arise from at least three different conflict types. First, the "world" that society would have defined as real may be at obvious and direct variance with scripture. Second, society's "world" may conflict with the corpus of theologically recognized natural law. Finally, there may be incongruities with the mystically received commands of God.

31. Berger, *The Sacred Canopy,* p. 99.

32. See Clarence L. Abercrombie, III, "Bases in Modern Protestant Theology for a Doctrine of Resistance to the Unjust State: Barth and Bonhoeffer." It should also be noted that, of the German academic faculties, only the theologians stood firm (fretted by few defections) against Hitler.

33. Berger, *The Sacred Canopy,* p. 100.

Chapter 2

PASTORS TO GOD'S CHOSEN PEOPLES:

A BRIEF SKETCH OF MILITARY CHAPLAINS

AND AMERICAN PREACHERS

And ye shall be unto me a kingdom of priests, and an holy nation.

Exodus 19:6

Maybe the religious leaders ought to realize that their total function is not only to enlighten their congregations, but to live with their parishioners and serve them and be aware of the values that are inherent in the community—instead of entering that community convinced of the need to instill a new set of values.

Spiro Agnew, on the American clergy

From the start both national reverence and Christian piety came to be seen as intrinsic elements in the religion of America. It thus became the duty of the churches to uphold the sacred trust and yet avoid the temptations of idolatry; to remind men of the country's ideals and yet preach that the God of Israel is a Judge of all nations. But in decade after decade the supreme difficulty of that task would be exhibited. Patriotism would protect and enliven the churches, yet threaten their integrity.

Sydney E. Ahlstrom

Since time immemorial men have cried out to powers beyond themselves for deliverance in time of trouble—and if you're fighting a war, you're frequently in a heap of trouble. Thus there probably were chaplains of a sort before the beginnings of recorded history. It is therefore not surprising that man's earliest religious chronicles are filled with tales of battles and of the mighty deeds of priests in those battles. One very ancient record of a religious hero's war role describes an incident from the thirteenth century BC. When Joshua led his troops against Amalek, Moses raised his arms above his head; maintaining this position, Moses infused the Israelite army with the spirit of Yahweh, thus ensuring their victory over the Amalekites (Exodus 17:11-13).

Later this function became more formalized. Yahweh commanded Moses to make two trumpets of beaten silver, to be used, among other things, as a battle signal: "And if ye go to war in your land against the enemy that oppresseth you, then ye shall blow an alarm with the trumpets; and ye shall be remembered before the LORD your God, and ye shall be saved from your enemies" (Numbers 10:9). The signal of the trumpets, it must be added, was not to be given by Moses himself, the Israelites' political-military leader. Instead it fell by Yahweh's command to the Aaronite priests by "a rule binding for all time."

The Bible makes it clear again and again that the religious functions of a military campaign were to be performed not by the military commander but by a man of God.[1] First stated during the time of Moses, this differentiation of what we might call a chaplain function remained explicit over the next 200 years, and indeed it was restated with especial firmness during the reign of Saul (1033?-1011? BC).[2] Throughout the remainder of the Old Testament, little more is said about the specific role of the priest or prophet in battle. Yet a biblical pattern had been set on which the role of chaplain could later be built.

The New Testament has often been interpreted as a pacifistic document. Strictly speaking, such a reading is probably inadequate, but it does not fall far wide of the mark. In the person of the Christ, heaven's kingdom was "at hand," already in the process of realizing God's ultimate triumph. In that final kingdom, war would be so obviously out of place that it merited no mention—not even condemnation—from Jesus. He had more important things to talk about.

The early Christians still felt very strongly that the imminent kingdom relegated to insignificance the things of this world, and (despite the ambiguity of much of the evidence that remains), it is clear that they generally refused to participate in the wars of Rome.[3] With so very few Christian soldiers, there was little need for Christian chaplains. In the reign of Emperor Constantine (312-337), however, Christianity changed almost overnight from an offbeat though somewhat popular religious sect to the established church of the greatest military power in the world. Followers of the Prince of Peace then entered military service in large numbers. Furthermore, though some censure was still attached to their participation, there can be no doubt that members of the clergy also served in the armies of Christian Rome.[4] It appears that some of those Roman "chaplains" took more than a vicarious interest in the physical conduct of military operations, and this attitude was even more evident among the priests who later accompanied the Crusades. The Council of Clermont (1095) had declared it the will of God that the holy sepulchre be recaptured and the heathen smitten. The priests were often glad to lend a hand:

A certain Latin priest stood on the stern and discharged arrows. Though streaming with blood, he was quite fearless ... at one and the same time he communicates the body and blood of God and becomes a man of blood, for this barbarian is no less devoted to sacred things than to war. This priest, or rather man of violence, wore his vestments while he handled an oar and was so bellicose as to keep on fighting after the truce.[5]

After the Crusades, things began to change. Especially in England, and to a certain extent in other European countries as well, soldiering came to be looked on not as an expression of God's will but rather as the business of the secular government—sometimes deadly, often dull, but always an affair to be regularized and disciplined as much as possible. Under such conditions the chaplain was not employed to exhort the men to greater heights of martial valor—English soldiers were expected to do their duty. Instead, the chaplain was present that he might minister to Christians who happened to be in the army. As early as 1350 the English chaplain's role was rather clearly defined, and the "fighting padre" had all but disappeared.[6] By 1600 the instructions to chaplains were explicit: "His duty is to have 'care of souls', and it is well if he meddle with no other business, but make that his only care."[7]

The militant Christians of Cromwell's armies brought about a temporary reversion to an earlier style of chaplaincy, but after the Restoration England's chaplaincy rapidly returned to normal.

Thus the chaplain who served British troops during the American Revolution was simply a priest to men in uniform. But his Patriot counterpart was something quite different; he was the trumpet of Jehovah, proclaiming a new crusade.[8] The reasons for this difference are both historical and theological. To begin, the American colonies were societal children of England's Reformation (which many colonists believed would lead to the complete purification of Christianity), and virtually all the most influential colony founders saw in the New World at least the chance to institutionalize those religious "gains" made in England under Puritan rule.[9] Some of the colonial founders, as we shall discover, wanted even more.

This book is certainly not the place for an analysis of England's seventeenth century "Reformation," but certain aspects of its theology bear so directly on American religious attitudes that we cannot escape a brief review. As in Europe, the Reformation in England placed great emphasis on study of the scriptures. Furthermore, this study was to be a sort of individual encounter with God's inspired word; it need *not* be done in the light of theological interpretations by the early church fathers. There developed as a result a most interesting interpretation of the Revelation of John. Radical Protestants, of course, had come to see the Roman papacy as the very incarnation of Satan, and they similarly looked on the Reformation as the beginning of Satan's defeat. They were also able to find biblical prophesy of just such an event in the twentieth chapter of Revelation:

> And I saw an angel come down from heaven, having the key of the bottomless pit and a great chain in his hand. And he laid hold on the dragon, that old serpent, which is the Devil, and Satan, and bound him a thousand years, and cast him into the bottomless pit, and shut him up, and set a seal upon him, that he should deceive the nations no more, till the thousand years should be fulfilled. (Revelation 20:1-3)

This passage, it is true, contained all the necessary images, but to bring it really "up to date" would require some fancy theologizing: To interpret the binding of Satan as an event of the sixteenth and seventeenth centuries that would be followed by an historical millennium of earthly bliss—such was to fly in the face of a thousand years of church doctrine, setting the Augustinian conception of history on its head. Saint Augustine had held that Satan was bound by the victorious resurrection of the Christ. The millennial promise of Revelation was thus interpreted allegorically: the "thousand-year" reign of Christ (which Augustine saw as identical to the "thousand-year" binding of Satan [10] and for which Augustine was probably unwilling to assign any human time limit) was accomplished not in the world at large but rather within the City of God.[11] The City of God now exists alongside of, even within, the City of the World (which is the abyss into which Satan was cast) and never attempts to take the world by force or to mold it as a whole into a godly shape; only God can do that, in the day that he establishes his final, complete kingdom on earth.[12] For Augustine, then, history has no ultimate goal toward which it can progress by means of human strivings: it will instead be fulfilled by God.

Despite the immense and ancient prestige of Augustinian theology, which endured to some extent even in the churches of the Reformation, some Protestant theologians were willing to challenge this philosophy of history. As I suggested earlier, they thought they had seen with their own eyes (in Wittenberg, in Geneva, in London) the defeat of the devil, and they were prepared to live in the millennium.[13] Furthermore, in the light of their millennial expectations, Protestant churchmen began to turn to the Old Testament. In it they found increasing support for their belief that secular history had meaning. And the Old Testament also tended to suggest that God realized that meaning *through the actions of a nation, a chosen people!*[14] Thus they came to believe that:

> If history is theodicy, if redemption is historical as well as individual, if evil is to be finally and decisively bound through great conflicts, God must operate through cohesive bodies of men; there must be children of light and children of darkness geographically, and the City of God and the City of the World should be susceptible of being designated on maps.[15]

Through the interweaving of three closely related theological themes, this religious concept of a chosen people reached its highest development in colonial New England. Millennialism, as we have seen, expressed the expectation of God's immediate earthly triumph. But how was this triumph to be accomplished? Luther, who was trained as an Augustinian monk,[16] felt that it was presumptuous even to ask such a question.[17] But another branch of the Reformation was prepared to offer some tentative answers. Since Calvin believed that the salvation of the elect had been foreordained, he was convinced that exposing people to God's immediate grace was less important than bringing them under discipline.[18] In Geneva as indeed in Massachusetts Bay,[19] it quickly became clear that the political components of such discipline were as important as the spiritual. Thus the Puritan "Calvinists" came to think in terms of applying discipline to the elect and the damned alike, of restructuring the nations according to the word of God![20]

It is in the light of this broad religiopolitical mission that we must understand the basic purpose of the Puritans who planted their colonies along the rugged coasts of Massachusetts and Connecticut,[21] and their ideas squarely in the heart of New England's theological movements. These hardy souls certainly did not set sail for the American wilderness for the sole purpose of separating themselves from the corruptions of the English churches. They felt, instead, that they were the true Church of England; separation had been the sin of others.[22] Still less did they come to found a country in which all people would have freedom of worship (as perhaps some of the *Mayflower's* Pilgrims had done).[23]

Instead, they wished to establish a "city on a hill," a "holy nation," a visible community of saints that could serve as a model for England and indeed the whole world to copy.[24]

Thus new interpretations of millennialism showed that God's kingdom could be established on earth, and the Puritans' "model" concept provided a means of establishment. Looking coldly back over three centuries, we may now find it paradoxical that Calvinism, according to which human beings lacked the power to affect their own salvation, gave rise to ideas that men and nations could bring in God's kingdom. However, for the Puritans themselves, this seeming paradox was neatly resolved through covenant theology. This, our third important religious theme, had its basis in the promises made by God to Abraham and to the Israelite nation (see, e.g., Genesis 15).[25] For Puritan theologians, covenants were first of all a way in which God in his distant majesty made his nature and will positively known.[26] Second, the covenant came to be interpreted as a contract; if man would keep his end of the bargain, God would keep his.[27]

Third, God's biblical covenants, into which the Puritans felt they had entered during the seventeenth century, generally promised, along with spiritual gifts, earthly blessings for the people who fulfilled their conditions.[28] Therefore, prosperity could frequently (though not always) be regarded as a sign of God's satisfaction,[29] and, conversely, misfortunes were generally evidence that God was not pleased with the way in which men were keeping their covenants.[30] Finally, the Puritans tended to emphasize not the personal but rather the sociopolitical dimensions of covenants[31]: Nations were thought to exist and prosper because of covenants with God to establish, on earth, his laws.[32]

In summary, from the early days of American colonization the Puritans had viewed their society as a chosen, covenanted nation that would serve as an active model for the earthly construction of Christ's millennial rule. Over the years, these ideas became more widely accepted, cutting across conventional religious and political lines; certain exceptions notwithstanding, Americans as a nation began to see themselves as a chosen people.[33] And American successes—which Preston would have called fruits of fulfilling the covenant, and Weber later termed the practical effects of piety[34]—often tended to support such an assumption.[35]

Thus (and I suppose we've taken a long theological sidetrack to see how) the groundwork for a militantly patriotic American church and chaplaincy was being laid from the beginning of New England's colonization. The settlers saw themselves as a new Israel, established as a model for the wicked homeland that was betraying its own Reformation.[36] "Bradford was 'our Moses,' and Winthrop 'our New-English Nehemiah.' When Bradford died, God raised up a 'Joshua' to lead 'our Israel' in its further pilgrimage."[37]

In America, this promised land, military activity was at first limited to campaigns against the heathen Indians, who fit quite well into the quasi-biblical allegory as "Canaanites."[38] The clergy (in good Old Testament form) were active in many of the "religious" campaigns of extermination. An early poem well expresses their spirit and zeal:

> Our worthy Captain Lovewell among them there did die;
> They killed Lieutenant Robbins, and wounded good young Frye,
> Who was our English chaplain; he many Indians slew,
> And some of them he scalpéd, when bullets round him flew.[39]

By the time of the Revolution the American colonists had carved out their "New Canaan" (witness the Connecticut town that bears that very name), and they were not willing to let apostate England reimpose its corrupt religion. Consequently, many clergymen were quick to support the war. Indeed, according to the official history of the Army Chaplain Corps, the words and deeds of the American clergy may have been largely responsible for persuading a wavering citizenry to support the cause of independence.[40]

Chaplains also served with the United States Army during the nineteenth century's wars of "manifest destiny." Especially interesting is the appointment of Roman Catholic priests to accompany the expedition against Mexico. Eugene McCormac states that this was done to prevent desertion among Irish conscripts, some of whom felt it was wrong to fight against their fellow Catholics south of the border.[41] The priests, McCormac argued, were appointed to show that the Lord was on the side of the United States.

In her early military struggles religious America had often seen the will of God. In the War Between the States she would find even more: It would be (for the North) the Great Crusade. Crusades, as modern scholars are well aware, are seldom generated instantaneously from crises of the moment; instead they tend to arise as the culmination of trends whose origins are far less visible than the final outbreak of violence. Such was certainly the case with our War Between the States.

We can now list a great many causes of that war. There was the constitutional question of the legality of secession; there was the early tariff; there was the whole business of states' rights; there was above all the political power struggle of two radically different socioeconomic formulas for national development. Nevertheless, *however important these and other similar factors may have been in bringing about the actual conflict, the issue of slavery contributed more directly to the war's significance as a crusade.*

The history of the churches' attack on slavery is quite complex, but the essential outline is not difficult to trace. In the early colonial period very little was said about slavery as an institution,[42] but during the last half of the eighteenth century a number of prominent church leaders were prepared to condemn it in no uncertain terms.[43] Such pronouncements, however, had very little apparent effect on the majority of the American people,[44] and the nineteenth century was well into its third decade before emancipation arose as a widely popular cause.[45] The reasons for this delayed reaction are not difficult to understand; until the turn of the century neither slavery nor Christianity was sufficiently widespread in the United States to cause a real confrontation. Times, however, changed! Eli Whitney's gin (patented 1794) spread the slave-based culture of cotton like wildfire across the South.[46] Meanwhile, the Great Revival (beginning about 1800) ushered into the United States a half-century of evangelical Christianity.[47]

The form of Christianity that flourished in nineteenth century America was at once the antithesis and the heir of Puritan theology. The doctrine of individual predestination, as Tocqueville realized, was never well suited to the democratic spirit of frontier America, and there eventually developed in its place the idea of free grace and the perfectibility of man.[48] (Such, of course, had been the doctrine of John Wesley, and it is not surprising that Methodism became the largest denomination in America.[49]) The rejection[50] of individual predestination doctrines did not, however, signal the collapse of Puritan ideas about the destiny of God's chosen America. Such ideas indeed took on increased importance:

> The Calvinist idea of foreordination, rejected as far as it concerned individuals, was now transferred to a grander object—the manifest destiny of a Christianized America. Men in all walks of life believed that the sovereign Holy Spirit was endowing the nation with resources sufficient to civilize the globe, to purge human society of all its evils, and to usher in Christ's reign on earth.[51]

There are thus two points in Professor Smith's perceptive passage that we must not miss: first is his observation that *Calvinist concepts of foreordination are now clearly applied to the nation* (as foreshadowed in the writings of John Preston); second is the idea that *national predestination involves the cleansing or perfection of society.* Grace and perfection, then, were the keynotes of the great revivals that spread the word of evangelical Christianity throughout the American North and West.[52] Naturally, much of the emphasis on "perfection" was in the direction of personal purity, but the ills of society were not to be left unattended. Revival preachers consistently attacked the idea of a personal perfection that lacked concern for the world,[53] and America's antebellum reform movements were to spring largely from evangelical Protestantism.[54] There were, of course, a number of reforms preached—temperance, education, women's and Indians' rights—*but the most important of all was the antislavery movement,*[55] *which came to overshadow and even to symbolize the need for all other forms of social change.*[56]

It was on this issue that the major religious traditions of the American North could unite,[57] and it was this issue that became a religious crusade; God's kingdom could come only with the purging of America's most despicable evil.[58] "Mine eyes have seen the glory of the coming of the Lord. . . ." Whether the biblical images were taken from Revelation 14:19-20 or from Revelation 19:11-16 or (as seems more likely) from a sort of general awareness of both, nothing could more explicitly illustrate the crusading spirit of the North than the great Battle Hymn. First of all, it was not written by some Bible-beating, backwoods preacher who could be expected to turn to the scriptures. Instead, it was composed by Julia Ward Howe, urbane, sophisticated, a contemporary of Emerson and Oliver Wendell Holmes (so far had the evangelical spirit of the millennial crusade spread). Second, the imagery is quite as clear as any in the book of Revelation.[59] Armageddon is at hand. God's historical purpose is to be fulfilled. Satan will at last be bound. And Christ himself appears on the scene:

11 And I saw heaven opened, and behold a white horse; and he that sat upon him was called Faithful and True, and in righteousness he doth judge and make war.
12 His eyes were as a flame of fire, and on his head were many crowns; and he had a name written that no man knew but he himself:
13 And he was clothed with a vesture dipped in blood: and his name is called, The Word of God.
14 And the armies which were in heaven followed him upon white horses, clothed in fine linen, white and clean.

15 And out of his mouth goeth a sharp sword, that with it he should smite the nations: and he shall rule them with a rod of iron: and he treadeth the wine-press of the fierceness and wrath of Almighty God.
16 And he hath on his vesture and on his thigh, a name written, KING OF KINGS, AND LORD OF LORDS. (Revelation 19:11-16)

And from the wine-press of God's wrath the blood did indeed flow, from Manassas to Appomattox, "even unto the horse-bridles, by the space of a thousand and six hundred furlongs" (Revelation 14:20). The North emerged from this war as a victorious crusader, with many convinced that the very carnage had served to purge the United States of her deepest blot of sin, that the pietistic cleansing emphasized since the days of the Puritans[60] had at last been fulfilled—in blood.[61] And America could at last take her place as the true New Israel.[62]

But if the North was the victorious crusader, molder of a promised land, what of the South? Surely in her defeat she developed some sense for the tragic ambiguity of human history? Unfortunately, it is generally true that she did not. First, the South could not know the complete tragedy of a defeated crusader because the war, for her, had never been exactly a crusade.[63] Second, though the South had lost the war, she somehow managed to win the "reconstruction," and she could point with pride to the preservation of "the Southern way of life" (increasingly a euphemism for institutionalized racism). Finally, the South slipped ever so rapidly back into the Union spirit,[64] striving to prove her loyalty and all-American patriotism. The Spanish-American War gave her the chance.[65]

As the War Between the States had been waged to make men free, the Spanish-American War was fought, as patriotic churchmen argued, to end the oppression of Cuba.[66] Next came World War I, prosecuted with equal vigor. Virtually all the American churches closed ranks, and Sydney Ahlstrom could quote a noted Unitarian who exclaimed he felt that Christ himself "would take bayonet and grenade and bomb and rifle and do the work of deadliness against that which is the most deadly enemy of his Father's Kingdom in a thousand years."[67] By the time we come to World War II (the crusade against Hitler[68]), the record of God's holy American wars has become almost tiring. Yet because the subject bears so directly on the chaplains I have examined, a few words must be said about the subsequent Cold War and its various warmer manifestations. We should start by recognizing that the Cold War, though militarily limited, was ideologically total. In the words of historian André Fontaine, it is, of all wars, "the first in which, beyond interests and passions, two recipes for automatic and universal happiness confront one another."[69]

The groundwork for the struggle had been laid long before Churchill's Iron Curtain speech (March 1946), before Yalta (February 1945), before World War II. Fontaine insists that any account of the conflict must begin with the history of the Russian Revolution, for it was in those years that the ideological battle lines between communistic Russia and the capitalistic West were drawn. And almost from the first the United States Army was deeply involved. Before the Communists had even consolidated their revolution, the United States joined the abortive allied expedition against the Reds in Siberia. The regimental crest of our 31st Infantry still carries the image of a polar bear to commemorate that bitter cold "Winter War." And the memories lingered. During the 1920s *Infantry Journal* (the most important semi-official publication of the army) carried numerous articles on the "Red Menace,"[70] and the American churches, with few exceptions, were equally ready to condemn the atheistic communists.[71]

Thus when the brief Soviet-American alliance of World War II came along, it was at best a marriage of necessity, and the end of the war, the inevitable divorce quickly ensued. Historians may argue forever about the reasons for Soviet expansion into Eastern Europe, but the American people, with their memories of Munich and their long-standing distrust of communism, generally interpreted this activity as a threat to world peace and freedom. The Soviet atomic tests, which ended American nuclear monopoly (September 1949), made the world situation appear even more threatening to Americans. They had always "known" that Russian Communists were untrustworthy, careless of human life, aggressive, and (worst of all) godless; but now there was a new factor. For the first time the Russians appeared to have the military capability to carry out some of their long-standing evil intentions! The reaction was understandable. One historian records:

> Ill-prepared for the complexities of foreign policy and the limitation on it, many people in the United States had come to regard the Soviet Union almost as the AntiChrist—Anti-communism emerged in the United States virtually as a secular religion. People viewed the world situation in rigid moral terms of right and wrong, Christian democracy and atheistic communism.[72]

As Professor Ahlstrom saw it,

> The chief religious result of the [post-World War II] international standoff was twofold. Consciously and subconsciously, with and without governmental stimuli, the patriotism of this "nation with the soul of a church" was aroused. Being a church member and speaking favorably of religion became a means of affirming the "American way of life," especially since the USSR and its Communist allies were formally committed to atheism. The other side of this process—and to a degree its result—was a long drawn out repetition of the Red Scare of 1919-20.[73]

It is hardly surprising that American churches took an important part in the ideological struggles of the Cold War. Were not the American armed forces (at least in the eyes of many citizen-Christians) all that stood between the church and a regime that was perceived as the worst persecutor of Christians since Nero's Rome? The churches rallied to the ideological defense of the "free world." Teaching nuns told parochial school children to prepare themselves for a possible martyrdom at the hands of the godless Russians. Methodist Youth Fellowships conducted innumerable programs of instruction on the evils of communism. Cardinal Spellman told soldiers in Vietnam (1966) that they were "fighting for Christ."[74] Once again, this time in Southeast Asia, the cause of America was identified with the will of God.[75]

In this chapter I have tried to show that until very recently most of the American churches have often supported United States military policy as the will of God. I have not wished to imply that our churches have sold out their Master to worship the United States and her wars. My purpose has been simply to demonstrate that chaplains for America's "crusades" could be recruited from the mainstream of American Christianity; it would not be necessary for the army to resocialize them or alter their values in any major way.

NOTES

1. See Numbers 31:6; II Chronicles 13:12-20.
2. See I Samuel 13:10-14.
3. This refusal to fight for Rome was also engendered in part by the requirement that a soldier take an oath to the emperor. Christians considered the oath to verge on idolatry.

4. Roland Bainton, *Christian Attitudes Toward War and Peace*, p. 88. One early Christian soldier was the humble Martin of Tours. On a long, dreary campaign into Gaul he met a beggar who seemed even colder and more miserable than the marching soldiers. Martin stopped long enough to rip in two his military cloak, giving half to the beggar and wearing the remainder as a cape. Martin had simply sought to help a fellow human being in need. But he became a saint, and his cape became a victory-totem, carried into battle by a special cape custodian, or *cappellanus*, from which word is derived the English *chaplain*. See Roy J. Honeywell, *Chaplains of the United States Army*, p. 5.

5. Quoted in Bainton, p. 114.
6. John Smyth, *In This Sign Conquer*, pp. xvii, 4.
7. Ibid., quoted on p. 14.
8. For reasons that will become apparent, this generalization is more apt for the New England (and perhaps even for the Middle Atlantic) colonies than for the South. See Sydney E. Ahlstrom, *A Religious History of the American People*, p. 196
9. Ibid., p. 123.
10. Augustine, *The City of God*, Book XX, Ch. 9.
11. Ibid., Book XX, Ch. 8.
12. Ibid., Book XX, Ch. 9; see also Book XV, Ch. I and Book XIX, Ch. 17.
13. Ernest Lee Tuveson, *Millennium and Utopia*, p. vii.
14. Tuveson, *Redeemer Nation*, pp. 27-29.
15. Ibid., p. 139.
16. Luther's training in the scholarly tradition of Augustinian monasticism (and Luther's consequent appreciation of the theology of Augustine himself) is emphasized by, for example, Edith Simon (see *Luther Alive*).
17. Luther placed more emphasis on the relationship of the individual to God within a world that would ever remain full of ambiguity.
18. Michael Walzer, *The Revolution of the Saints*, p. 51.
19. Edmund S. Morgan, *The Puritan Dilemma*, p. 163; see also Richard L. Bushman, *From Puritan to Yankee*, pp. 147 ff.
20. Walzer, p. 1.
21. Here we will be talking primarily about the Massachusetts Bay Company, the New Haven colony, and (to a lesser extent) the Connecticut colony. See Morgan, *The Puritan Dilemma*, p. 187, and *Visible Saints*, pp. 107-108
22. The Puritans were extremely sensitive about the issue of separatism, which they condemned as schism and sin. See Morgan, *The Puritan Dilemma*, especially pp. 51, 115, and Perry Miller, *Errand into the Wilderness*, p. 14.
23. Freedom of religion was precisely contrary to the Puritan idea that elect and damned alike should be brought under godly discipline:

> To allow no dissent from the truth was exactly the reason they had come to America. They maintained here precisely what they had maintained in England, and if they exiled, fined, jailed, whipped, or hanged those who disagreed with them in New England, they would have done the same thing in England could they have secured power. (Miller, "Puritan State and Puritan Society," from *Errand into the Wilderness*, p. 145.)

See also Morgan's *Visible Saints*, pp. 106 ff.

24. Miller, *Errand into the Wilderness,* pp. 48, 69; and Christine A. Hope, "Town Development and Social Change in Colonial Connecticut," pp. 4-5.
25. Walzer, p. 168.
26. Miller, "The Marrow of Puritan Divinity," in *Errand into the Wilderness,* pp. 60-61, 71.
27. John Preston, *The New Covenant,* pp. 315-316. See also Miller, "The Marrow of Puritan Divinity."
28. Preston, pp. 107-108, 381-382.
29. Morgan, *The Puritan Dilemma,* p. 70.
30. Miller, *Errand into the Wilderness,* p. 8; any misfortune, from excess caterpillars to Indian wars to bad children, might be regarded as a sign of God's displeasure.
31. Walzer, p. 170.
32. Morgan, *The Puritan Dilemma,* p. 19.
33. Tuveson, *Redeemer Nation,* pp. xiii-x, 53-54; see also Ahlstrom, *A Religious History of the American People,* p. 80.
34. See Preston; and Max Weber, *The Protestant Ethic and the Spirit of Capitalism.*
35. See Ahlstrom, "The American National Faith," pp. 105-106.
36. See Miller, *Errand into the Wilderness,* p. 18; Walzer, p. 150; Morgan, *The Puritan Dilemma,* p. 48.
37. Winthrop S. Hudson (Ed.), *Nationalism and Religion in America,* pp. 7, 33.
38. George H. Williams, "The Chaplaincy in the Armed Forces of the United States of America in Historical and Ecclesiastical Perspective," in Harvey G. Cox (Ed.), *Military Chaplains,* p. 15.
Perry Miller and Thomas H. Johnson, *The Puritans,* Vol. I, pp. 143-144, 146-152, and especially pp. 161-162.
Michael McGiffert, *Puritanism and the American Experience,* pp. 160, 167-168, and especially pp. 175-176.
39. Honeywell, p. 18.
40. Ibid., p. 35. See also Ahlstrom, *A Religious History of the American People,* p. 361.
41. Eugene McCormac, *James K. Polk,* p. 421. Honeywell (pp. 83-84) denies this allegation; he holds that the priests were sent to Mexico to calm the Mexican population, which feared religious persecution. Neither side of this debate claims that the priests were appointed primarily to serve the spiritual needs of the soldiers, and yet it seems that the priests themselves saw such duties as constituting their proper role.
42. See Louis Filler, *The Crusade Against Slavery,* p. 1. In addition, the opposition that did exist did not generally come from the clergy. Instead, it appears that the political leaders, especially in the state of Virginia (Filler, p. 10), should receive more credit.
43. One of the major critics was Thomas Coke, John Wesley's personal emissary to the American churches. See Warren T. Smith, *Thomas Coke and Early American Methodism,* pp. 202 ff. Donald G. Matthews (*Slavery and Methodism,* p. 19) indicates that by 1795 Methodist ministers in Virginia and South Carolina were resolved neither to own slaves nor to allow the ordination of slaveholders.
44. Filler, p. 1.

45. Ibid., p. 10.
46. Between 1791 and 1803, cotton exports increased by nearly 20,000%! (See *The Lincoln Library of Essential Information*, p. 2003.)
47. Morgan, "Ezra Stiles and Timothy Dwight," pp. 101-102.
48. Alexis de Tocqueville, *Democracy in America*, pp. 156-158. Similarly, Edmund Morgan (see "The Marrow of Puritan Divinity," especially pp. 80-83) has argued that the Puritans themselves were prone to put much less stress on the doctrine of predestination than we might have expected. Suffice it to say that the temptation to flirt with Arminianism has been persistently strong in most American denominations.
49. The Baptists, who held second place in membership statistics, often tended to follow quite closely the doctrine if not the ecclesiastical structure of their Methodist brethren. And by 1855, Methodists and Baptists together comprised about 70% of United States Protestants. (See Timothy L. Smith, *Revivalism and Social Reform*, p. 22.)
50. See Joseph R. Gusfield, "Temperance, Status Control, and Mobility, 1826-60," in David B. Davis (Ed.), *Ante-Bellum Reform*, p. 127. It should be obvious, however, that religious trends seldom if ever carry everyone along in their new waves.
51. T. L. Smith, p. 7.
52. A major thesis of T. L. Smith's book is that contrary to popular belief, nineteenth century revivalism was of more lasting import in the cities of the North than in any other portion of the country. Significantly, revivalism did not catch on in the South until the early 1860s—and the coming of the war (T. L. Smith, pp. 77-78). It should also be noted (and one is tempted to correlate this fact with the absence of evangelical-perfectionist revivalism) that the churches in the South were generally concerned with the spiritual welfare of the Negro only; sermons to slaves often insisted that they should be content with their lot. (See Matthews, pp. 78, 83.)
53. T. L. Smith, p. 157.
54. Davis, p. 1.
55. T. L. Smith, pp. 108, 153, 223.
56. Ibid., p. 200, and Davis, p. 2.
57. T. L. Smith, pp. 82-85, 108, and (especially) 181.
58. Ibid., p. 225, see also Filler, p. 33.
59. See Charles M. Laymon (Ed.), *The Interpreter's One-Volume Commentary on the Bible*, pp. 965-966.
60. See Ahlstrom, "The American National Faith," pp. 105-106.
61. Tuveson, *Redeemer Nation*, pp. 162-163. In my opinion, any theological interpretation that emphasizes the purging of sin only through human blood and suffering stands in heretical contrast to the central Christian message that the suffering of Jesus Christ was sufficient to overcome all sin.
62. Although the spirit of reform lingered in some areas (later to be revived in the Social Gospel movement), the freeing of the slaves removed "the central hub of reform," and the driving unity of the reformers was ended (Filler, p. xv). Essentially they felt that their greatest work had been done. For a time the churches were rather active in the business of reconstruction, but they missed many opportunities, and after the woefully premature "compromise" of 1876, the South and the Negro were forgotten—even the Social Gospel did not revive their memory (Ahlstrom, *A Religious History of the American People*, p. 691).

63. It is certainly true that the South had seen the war as a righteous defense of "property" and home; it was viewed as a just war, a *very* just war, but not as a crusade. See Williams, in Cox (Ed.), p. 33.

64. Yet perhaps the South should have spent a bit more time in meditation on her past sins and her terrible defeat. She rushed *so* wholeheartedly, with very few exceptions, back into the arms of the Union. It was almost as if the South felt obliged to beg forgiveness from the conquering Yankees instead of taking the proper Christian course of (1) accepting God's forgiveness and then (2) working for justice and for eventual forgiveness from the Negro! (See C. Vann Woodward, *The Burden of Southern History;* it is a tragedy that this great book was published only after it was almost too late for the South to learn the lessons it teaches.)

65. Kenneth M. MacKenzie, for example, mentions "the scene of General Wheeler, a former soldier in gray, riding onto the battlefield of Chickamauga to take command of a cavalry division of the United States Army [for service in Cuba], this time in a uniform of blue." See *The Robe and the Sword,* p. 79.

66. Honeywell, p. 58. Ahlstrom (in *A Religious History of the American People)* states, "The united evangelical front closed ranks for . . . the Little War of 1898" (p. 8), and "As it turned out, America loved the splendid little war.' . . . The church reflected the American consensus—and then proceeded in the limited time available to convert the war into a crusade and to rationalize imperialism as a missionary obligation" (p. 879). MacKenzie's *The Robe and the Sword* describes at length how the Methodists, then America's largest denomination, supported the Spanish-American War as well as the extensions of the American "empire" that followed. For the Methodists, the oppression of Cuba was the chief reason used to justify the war. (See MacKenzie, especially pp. 50-58, 63, 67, 71.) Certainly there was some opposition to the war, especially in the Northeast, but especially once the fighting had begun, it is difficult to find any record of serious opposition from within the churches. In general, even the Roman Catholics supported the war wholeheartedly (Ahlstrom, *A Religious History of the American People,* p. 880).

67. Ahlstrom, *A Religious History of the American People,* p. 885; see also p. 8.

68. The American churches did offer their full support to this war, yet their response, like that of the American people as a whole, was more reasoned—and less ranting—than it had been during World War I (ibid., p. 949). This complete yet reasoned response had been untiringly advocated by church leaders such as Reinhold Niebuhr (Donald B. Meyer, *The Protestant Search for Political Realism,* especially pp. 349-403).

69. André Fontaine, *History of the Cold War,* Vol. I, p. 7.

70. See Abercrombie, "Politicization."

71. Ahlstrom, *A Religious History of the American People,* p. 900.

72. Athan G. Theoharis, *The Yalta Myths,* p. 72.

73. Ahlstrom, *A Religious History of the American People,* pp. 951-952.

74. Williams, in Cox (Ed.), p. 53.

75. Since the mid-1960s, this religious support for America and her wars may have been declining, as I hope to show in a later chapter. See Ahlstrom, "The American National Faith," pp. 123-124; see also Ahlstrom, "The American National Faith: Where Did It Go?" p. 8.

Chapter 3

FROM SAMPLE SELECTION TO PAPER-SHREDDERS, OR THE HARD MECHANICS OF RESEARCHING THE CHAPLAINCY

A NOTE FROM THE UNDERGROUND
by Nonrespondent No. 5542

The little men in untold legions,
Descend upon the private regions.
Behold my child, the questionnaire.
And be as honest as you dare.

"As briefly as possibly, kindly state
Age and income, height and weight.
Sex (M or F); sex of spouse
(spouses—list).

      Do you own your house?
How much of your income goes for rent?
Give racial background, by percent.
Have you had, or are you now having
Orgasm? Or thereunto a craving?
Will Christ return? If so, when?
(Kindly fill this out in pen.)
Do you masturbate? In what style?
(Fill and return the enclosed vial.)
Do you eat, or have you eaten
Feces? Whose?

      And were you beaten?
Was your mother? sister? dog?
(Attach descriptive catalogue.)
Have you mystic inspiration?
Our thanks for your co-operation."

Distended now with new-got lore,
Our plump and pleasant men-of-war
Torture whimsey into fact,
And then, to sanctify the act,

Cast in gleaming, ponderous rows,
Ingots of insipid prose.
A classic paper! Soon to be,
Rammed down the throats of such as we.

(Written anonymously in lieu of a returned questionnaire for Demerath-Lutterman study of campus religion and student values, University of Wisconsin, 1972.)

To my knowledge, there is no hard and fast rule requiring a social science text to be boring, but seemingly the very subject matter of such books calls for at least one chapter that strains the patience of the reader and drives the writer straight up the walls. So to my readers I offer warning: This chapter is the worst! And yet I must temper one warning with another: He who does not read this chapter and understand the hard mechanics of my research methodology will be left at loose ends as he passes through the remaining chapters. I shall be brief as possible, however, and shall relegate to the appendices material that is not directly necessary to an understanding of this work's main thrust.

In the beginning it was my plan to study the military chaplaincy in detail to see whether "the chaplain" tended to legitimate military goals and missions or, instead, acted as an independent, "prophetic" (to use the theological term) voice within the military establishment. Originally I hoped to spend a lot of time talking intensively with a relatively small number of chaplains, observing them in their work, and attempting to define their theological and sociological role position within the military environment. For three reasons I decided to abandon such a strategy. First, it became increasingly clear that I would not have the opportunity to work with and observe chaplains on a day-to-day basis. The air force and the navy reacted almost hostilely to the very idea, and the army, though extremely cordial, pointed out many military and religious factors that would foredoom the research proposed for anyone but a true participant-observer (i.e., a chaplain).

Second, even my preliminary research convinced me that there was no such animal as "the chaplain." There were men—ministers, priests, rabbis—who carried the president's commission, and though their role as chaplains certainly influenced their actions and attitudes, they remained altogether too individual for me to lump into one batch. I was thus afraid that if I observed only a small sample, I could draw no general conclusions. To put it statistically, with chaplains (as, perhaps, with graduate students or professors) all the standard deviations are unacceptably large.

There remains a third reason for my abandoning the interview-a-few-chaplains strategy: It had been done too often already. In searching the literature I came across two "sociological" books on the chaplaincy, two dissertations, one incredibly lengthy master's thesis, and a great many "popular" books and articles. Each of these works was interesting, in its own way, but all shared a crucial flaw. Chaplains were viewed in isolation; no attempts were made to relate them to a broader theological or military context.[1]

In summary, I was unable to interview and observe chaplains directly; I was reluctant to touch a small sample; and I wanted to look at chaplains as part of a bigger picture. Thus the parameters of a feasible research project were being set by choice and by necessity, and eventually I came up with a design that within its limits has worked rather well.

DEFINING POPULATIONS FOR STUDY

I decided to attack the problem with a mailed questionnaire. Because the chaplaincy was to be the major focus of my research, I concentrated on defining my sample of chaplains. Since I had already discovered that I could not lump all chaplains together into one batch, the problem became one of selecting categories. Denomination was a major key. Although I lacked the resources to study all the chaplains, I could select my sample by denominations. But which denominations should I choose? For a time it seemed that the problem was out of my hands. The office of the Chief of Chaplains had refused to supply a list of chaplains' addresses and had suggested that I obtain the information from the endorsing agencies[2] of the civilian denominations. I acquired a number of addresses in that way, mostly from the smaller denominations; the larger civilian churches (1) had developed rules preventing disclosure of addresses or (2) were too busy to respond. Then I got some real help from a Southern Baptist official: No, he was sorry; he couldn't give me his list of addresses, but why didn't I get my addresses the way the Baptists get theirs? Simply send one dollar to the Chaplain School book department and request a chaplains' roster. This was quickly done, and I received, by return mail, a 1972 roster, with the address of every army chaplain then on active duty. So I selected my denominations on criteria other than necessity, limiting my study to

Lutherans, Roman Catholics, Southern Baptists, and United Methodists. These denominations were chosen, first, because they are the most numerous both in American society and in the Army Chaplains Corps (about 65% of all army chaplains belong to one of these four denominations). Second, the denominations have quite different organizational structures. The Catholics have a rigid episcopal system under the ultimate leadership of the pope. Similarly, the Methodists, though protestants, are very tightly organized at the conference level (about two conferences per state), but they lack a single, overall head. The individual Lutheran parishes are more nearly independent than are the Methodists, and the Southern Baptists have only a loosely structured denominational organization. Also, the denominations justify Christian participation in war in different ways. The Methodists and Baptists, by doctrine, hold that war is generally reprehensible but that the conscience of an individual Christian (when guided by God) can direct participation in military action. Catholicism developed the idea of the "just war," fulfilling certain specific conditions, in which Christian participation is acceptable. The Lutheran church preserved much of the Catholic doctrine, though it often laid more stress on the right of the state to define the conditions of a just war. I expected that all these denominational differences would be crucial variables in determining the relationship of a chaplain to his military environment.[3] I would mail a questionnaire to every army chaplain in each of my subject denominations (N = 984).[4]

Having designated my chaplain sample, my next task became the definition of a broader framework within which to study the roles and opinions of those chaplains. I therefore attempted to define a continuum of role and value expectations, stretching from those of civilian denominations (which educate and endorse the chaplains) to those of military officers (who command the chaplains and fill out their efficiency reports).

It was quite simple to define my population of military commanders; I decided to send a questionnaire to every military officer in command of a unit to which a Methodist, Catholic, Lutheran, or Southern Baptist army chaplain was assigned as of 1 January 1972 (N = 447).[5]

I chose to define the role expectations and values of the civilian denominations chiefly by sending questionnaires to their civilian priests and ministers. I utilized a table of random units to generate from nationwide lists a sample of 100 clergymen for each denomination (total, N = 400).[6]

Questionnaire Design

While I was trying to get my samples straight,[7] I was also working to develop my survey instrument. Although I wanted similar information from each of my three populations, I realized quite early that I would need three separate questionnaires. Therefore, in the spring of 1972, I wrote out three pilot questionnaires and conducted an initial in-house "testing" with friends of mine (graduate students, faculty members, clergymen, and military officers). All approved of the basic design, but all made the following comments: (1) "Your questionnaires are much *too long*," and (2) "You should *add* the following questions." After much detailed revision, three pilot questionnaires were mailed in early June to the following samples of military officers, army chaplains, and civilian clergymen.

Pilot Questionnaire for Military Officers. This questionnaire was sent to 30 military officers drawn at random from the telephone directory of Fort Benning, Georgia. (Warrant officers and lieutenants were systematically excluded.) Eleven questionnaires (37%) were returned.

Pilot Questionnaire for Army Chaplains. This questionnaire was sent to 30 active-duty army chaplains of the following denominations[8]:

1. Lutheran   10 chaplains
2. Presbyterian (northern branch)   5 chaplains
3. United Church of Christ   5 chaplains
4. Disciples of Christ   5 chaplains
5. Episcopalian   5 chaplains

Eleven questionnaires (37%) were returned.

Pilot Questionnaire for Civilian Clergymen. This questionnaire was sent to 30 civilian clergymen of the following denominations:

1. Lutheran   10 clergymen
2. Presbyterian (northern branch)   5 clergymen
3. United Church of Christ   5 clergymen
4. Disciples of Christ   5 clergymen
5. Episcopalian   5 clergymen

The denominations and numbers had, of course, been chosen to parallel those of the pilot survey chaplains. Seventeen questionnaires (56%) were returned.

The results of the pilot questionnaires were most instructive in two respects. First and most important, they presented substantive data that forced me to reevaluate the very hypotheses I had chosen to study. I had expected to find in chaplains a conflict of value sets associated with their roles as both clergymen and military officers. In one key question I asked about attitudes toward values. The chaplains were requested to indicate how each of 30 value-laden attributes would be evaluated by (1) a man ideal for the role of military officer and (2) a man ideal for the role of Christian clergyman. Answers varied among chaplains, but the interesting finding was this: *Every* chaplain saw clerical and military role values as being almost identical! Thus the focus of my major survey instrument had to be changed; I decided not to concentrate on the extent of "role conflict" among chaplains, since it was so small, but rather to concentrate on the ways in which each chaplain defines his (relatively conflict-free) role.

The second finding I drew from the pilot survey was that all three populations—military officers, chaplains, and civilian clergymen alike— were considerably more sensitive to the questions I wished to ask than had been my friends and advisors. Questions that had appeared quite innocent to me were perceived by my pilot respondents to be biased or even grossly insulting. I took great pains to remedy this defect in my major instrument, but as we shall see I was not completely successful.

My final questionnaires (see Appendix) were developed over the summer of 1972. Their physical format was professional, and they were mass-duplicated by a photo-offset method. The questionnaires for civilian clergymen and military officers were four pages long; the questionnaire for the chaplains ran to eight pages. After consultation with my advisors (particulary Professor Donald Ploch) I decided to make two mailings.

To be sure that those who had filled out the first questionnaire would not be bothered with a second, I attached a code number to each questionnaire of the first mailing.[9] I explained in my cover letters (see Appendix) that I would make no attempt to connect names with questionnaire responses. Furthermore, I decided that in general I should refrain from connecting unit identities with specific responses, for this was a concern of some chaplains and military commanders. The questionnaires were sent out as first-class mail in Yale University, Department of Political Science, envelopes. Respondents were provided with a business reply envelope addressed to me, care of the Department of Political Science.[10]

From Sample Selection to Paper-Shredders [53]

Return Rates

It ought to be easy enough to report return rates. Simply divide the number of questionnaires returned by the number sent out, multiply the result by 100%, and report the figure, perhaps in a footnote. Unfortunately, nothing involving the church, the army, and the postal service can be so simply accomplished.

I sent out 984 questionnaires to chaplains, 447 to military commanders, and 400 to clergymen. Let us first consider the clergymen, since they are the least complicated. Two had died, thus cannot be faulted for failing to return their questionnaires. One neither spoke nor read English, and one was not a clergyman at all (she was a nun who had somehow been listed in the Catholic priests' register). From the first mailing, 10 additional letters were returned as undeliverable. On that first mailing, 130 questionnaires (of 386 otherwise unaccounted-for questionnaires) were filled out. On the second mailing, 256 questionnaires were sent out. Seven were returned as undeliverable, and 42 were returned completed. We can calculate a return rate from the 172 filled out and the 386 presumably delivered at least once; that rate would be about 44%.

My first mailing to unit commanders consisted of 447 questionnaires, addressed not to individuals but rather to positions (e.g., "Commanding Officer, 4th U.S. Army Missile Command"). The list of units had been drawn up in late 1971, and by late 1972 many of the Vietnam-based units had been disbanded or deactivated. Thirty-three questionnaires were returned unopened for that reason, leaving 414 presumably delivered in the first mailing. Of these, 102 were returned completed. On the second mailing, about 312 questionnaires were sent out; 20 were returned untouched because of further unit deactivations; 51 were returned filled out.[11] Of the 414 questionnaires presumably delivered at least once, 153 were returned, for a rate of about 37%.

The chaplains are the most difficult group to handle. On the first mailing, consisting of 984 questionnaires, 44 were returned as undeliverable, and 266 were filled out. Of those that were presumably delivered, 43 of the addressees had been discharged from the army. From my second mailing, 103 questionnaires were returned as undeliverable, and 81 were returned in completed form. Thus we could calculate a return rate of 39% from the total returns (347) and the total presumably delivered at least once to chaplains (897).

I would have been willing to leave my reporting of return rates at that if I had not heard from a friend who said he had mailed a completed questionnaire to me. Since I had not received the questionnaire, I wondered how many more might have been lost in the mail. I therefore sent out a postcard questionnaire to a random sample of 100 chaplains from whom I had not received completed questionnaires. The following data gained from that sample are of interest at this point:

Replies	Number
"I am no longer a chaplain."	3
"I never received your questionnaire."	6
"I did return your questionnaire."	3

If we can extrapolate from that random sample, perhaps we can assume that among the 550 chaplains from whom I had not received completed questionnaires, there were (a) 17 men who were no longer chaplains, (b) 33 chaplains who had never received a questionnaire, and (c) 17 chaplains who had returned questionnaires that were subsequently lost in the mail. We can eliminate the chaplains and former chaplains in categories (a) and (b) from our original population and add the chaplains in (c) to the "returned" column; then we can calculate a hypothetical return rate of about 43%. I do not report this to artificially inflate my return rates; the reader knows what the "real," in-hand rate was: 39%. Moreover, I have more than enough returned chaplain questionnaires (in raw numbers) to perform valid statistical manipulations; I could have done quite well with half as many. I am more concerned, however, about the possible bias that could be indicated by an excessively low return rate. When we see that about 43% of the questionnaires would have been returned if the mechanics of mailing had worked more smoothly, perhaps our confidence will be increased. Furthermore, a quick glance at some of the political science literature based on mailed surveys seems to indicate that even a 39% return rate is not at all bad. For his doctoral thesis at Yale University, Roy E. Licklider mailed to 491 "private nuclear strategists" questionnaires that were similar in length (and to a degree, in subject matter) to mine. After two mailings he achieved a return rate of just under 39%.[12] And James Rosenau is even more generous in his definition of a good return rate: "A return of one-quarter of the questionnaires is generally considered to be a high response and often, depending on the subject and the respondents, the return rate may not be more than five or ten per cent."[13]

I am thus willing to conclude that in at least two respects, my return rates were adequate: I had more than enough raw data to apply the statistical procedures I deemed appropriate, and my return rates were no lower than those of other political scientists who had utilized mailed surveys and found their results satisfactory.

Bias

It is difficult to comment definitively about the possible bias of the data I have in hand. If there were some technique enabling the precise determination of the presence or extent of a possible bias, I would have used that magical method to gather *all* my data and never would have resorted to the worrisome, expensive questionnaires. Nevertheless, I can say a few words on the general subject.

First, there were a number of people who did not like my questionnaires at all. These individuals were not limited to any one of the professions but rather had their representatives among the clergymen, chaplains, and commanders alike. Some thought the questionnaire was academically deficient. Others felt that a study such as mine, made at the present time, could be harmful to the church, the chaplaincy, or the army. These criticisms I could easily understand; I admit that when I was on active duty, I would have hesitated to fill out such a questionnaire. One could even laugh at the case of the questionnaire that had been run through a classified documents shredder! Yet I was personally hurt by the comments of a few military officers who thought I was out to attack the army. I certainly was no war hero; I don't even claim to have been an especially proficient officer. But I do love the dear old Green Machine, and if push finally came to shove, I'd put my life on the line again for the army. Anyhow, one commander's letter touched all the bases, and I'd feel singularly gutless if I failed to quote it in full:

Dear Sir:

Reference your second letter to me and your dissertation on the Army Chaplaincy.

I hoped by my abstention you would have rationalized that the questionnaire was not worth the effort to complete. I do not care if your survey is biased, pointed, inadequate, narrow and totally incomplete and incompetent.

Questions 18 thru 25 really don't fit the bill as to the chaplaincy of the United States Army. Nationalism vs. a united world? My honor? Population centers? Qualities of war? The military profession? These are subjects within themselves and are personal and universal in content and substance.

I respect those military officers who have not responded to your questionnaire and I have concern for the apparent stupidity of those who did. I fear your assumed expertise of your old Army days and your already developed biasness to same.

I wish you luck in your dissertation and hope very much that it will be published in *LIFE* magazine, if not, I know *RAMPARTS* will publish it. "GO IVY LEAGUE!"[14]

With such comments, one would be inclined to suspect a definite bias among my nonreturners. I can state, however, that many of those who filled out the questionnaire were equally harsh in their condemnation:

> This is the worst form I ever filled out. Your bias (sic) attitude shows over all of it. I hope you some day get an education.[15]

> I got the impression from the flavor of your question that you do not think very highly of chaplains.[16]

> You are too damn patronizing in your approach. You turned me off.[17]

> Many of the questions are loaded. I am only doing this because I believe that besides being with 101st you were also with me in 1st BDE, 5th (MECH), at Quang Tri.[18]

These quotes clearly show that I received completed questionnaires not only from people who liked the apparent focus of my research but also from those who opposed it. Furthermore, I received a large number of replies from chaplains who felt for me a sense of unit camaraderie because they too had served in the 101st Airborne Division: "I was your chaplain in Vietnam, so I am glad to help you. I wish people in all the world would accept the true principles of Christianity and there would not be any wars [signed, Former 101st ABN DIV]."[19] A half-dozen other chaplains mentioned in response to specific questions that they had been with the 101st, and still others wrote in the margin things like "101st All the way ... 502nd First Strike 1965-1967."[20] Thus some respondents filled out the questionnaire even though they didn't like it, and the "Screaming Eagles"—front line as well as division support chaplains—returned it en masse. I therefore think I received a sample of returns adequate for my study.

My next strategy in the attempt to check for bias involved the fact that I had sent out two questionnaire mailings. It seemed logical to expect that those who responded only after I had contacted them a second time were somewhat more reticent about answering than those who had replied to my first mailing. I reasoned that second-mailing respondents would be more like nonrespondents than would those who had answered my first communication. Thus *significant differences between first- and second-mailing responses might be indicative of return bias.* As it turned out, for the commanders and civilian clergymen the differences between the two mailings were very small; for the chaplains there were no noticeable differences.

We have found it useful, then, to examine returned data in order to say something about its bias, and thus far the results of all our tests have been most encouraging. Now it is advisable to peek a glimpse, however fragmentary, of the members of the population who found it most convenient to slip the questionnaires into their wastebaskets. In the cases of the civilian clergymen and military commanders, this is simply impossible; I have no more data than the return rates already presented. For the chaplains, however, something more can be done. As I have stated, the "chaplain roster" contains, besides addresses, the age, rank, and denomination of each chaplain on active duty. Therefore, I decided to take these data vectors as independent variables and see how they affected a dependent variable, return/nonreturn of questionnaires. I reasoned that if my return rate were greatly influenced by these background variables, I would have to be especially wary in subsequent analyses.

I therefore formulated what was, in essence, a regression-type model,

$$R = a + b_1 A + b_2 G + b_3 D$$

where R = return "rate"
a = a constant intercept term
b = constant regression coefficients
A = age
G = military grade, or rank
D = denomination

The age variable was arrived at as follows. The oldest chaplain in my population was born in 1911. I took his birthyear and gave it the value "0"; similarly, I gave 1912 the value "1," 1913 the value "2," and so on, through the youngest chaplain's birthyear, 1947, which was given the value "36." Thus A = [birthyear−1911].

I gave the denomination with the highest return rate (the Methodists) a D-value of "0"; the denomination with the lowest return rate (the Catholics) was given a "3," and so on:

    for United Methodists $D = 0$
    for Southern Baptists $D = 1$
    for Lutherans $D = 2$
    for Roman Catholics $D = 3$

For ranks, I gave the lowest-ranking chaplains (captains) a G-value of "0." Majors received a "1," and so on, up through the Chief of Chaplains (a major general) who received a "5":

    for captain $G = 0$
    for major $G = 1$
    for lieutenant colonel $G = 2$
    for colonel $G = 3$
    for brigadier general $G = 4$
    for major general $G = 5$

As stated previously, the bias-examination model was essentially a regression-type problem. Certain factors, however, preclude the application of a straight regression approach. First, if we wish to think in terms of return "rates," we have a dependent variable bounded at 0% and 100%. Thus (and visualize, for example, the bivariate case) we could expect a line describing the relationship of two variables to behave asymptotically as it approached the 0% and 100% limits. If this were the only problem, it could be handled easily enough by a logit transformation. However, we must remember that my R-data really present no rates at all; rather, they comprise a dichotomous variable that has only two values, "not returned" or "returned" (to which I have assigned values of "0" and "1," respectively). This was a problem for probit analysis (which for the moment can be described as a modified regression technique capable of dealing with the problems of my bias-examination data set).

First I ran a multivariate probit analysis with age, rank, and denomination as independent variables. Tests of statistical "significance" revealed that *only age influenced the return rates to an extent appreciably greater than chance*. A further test showed that rank and denomination taken together still had no "significant" effect.[21] Let us therefore concentrate our analysis on the age variable, which yielded a probit coefficient "significant" at the .05 level. Here we shall examine the bivariate probit analysis of R on A (which has at least the virtue of being less messy to explain than a multivariate form).

Probit coefficients are basically analogous to regression coefficients, and their units are of a standard normal form.[22] These two basic points should become clear as we discuss the probit equation for return on age:

$$R = -0.78 + 0.02A.$$

The R may be interpreted as follows. (1) R will define a cutoff point on a standard normal curve (mean = 0; standard deviation = 1). (2) The percentage of the curve to the left of the cutoff point will be our best guess of the percentage of chaplains, age A_i, who returned the questionnaire. The -0.78 is an intercept term, given in standard deviation form. The $+0.02A$ says that for each increase in A (i.e., for every year between 1911 and a chaplain's birthyear—for every year *younger* a chaplain happens to be), R will increase by $+0.02$ standard deviation units.

I shall illustrate with two examples. First, let us look at a hypothetical set of chaplains born in 1911. For them, A is 0; thus $R = -0.78$. Looking up -0.78 in a table of the normal curve, we find that about 22% of the chaplains could be expected to return the questionnaire. Now let us consider chaplains born 20 years later, in 1931. Here we must calculate

$$R = -0.78 + 0.02(20)$$
$$R = -0.38$$

About 35% of these younger chaplains could be expected to return the questionnaire. To get some idea of the range of the effect of age on return rates, we take hypothetical groups of chaplains representing the oldest and youngest members of my population:

Age of Chaplains	Expected Return Rate
61 (born 1911, oldest)[23]	22%
25 (born 1947, youngest)	48%

Thus it seems at first glance that the effect of age on return rate is more than just *statistically* significant; there is a whopping difference between 22% and 48%. Yet to be sure that we do not exaggerate the effect, let us focus our bias examination on the age group that contains about two-thirds of the chaplains in my population:

Age of Chaplains	Expected Return Rate
49	30%
43 (born 1929, mean age)	34%
37	38%

Here the difference is certainly much smaller—and much less frightening. Furthermore, some data I have received from the Chaplain School[24] indicates that a number of the very oldest chaplains had retired before the questionnaire was sent out. These former chaplains did not receive the questionnaire, yet because full information on this is not available, they were included in my probit analysis as "received but did not return." Thus the age bias may not be as strong as the probit coefficients indicate.

Interestingly, other social scientists have had the same problem of age bias on questionnaire returns. Licklider, for example, also found that the older members of his population were much less likely to return questionnaires.[25] It is not altogether clear why this should be the case; my own research, inconclusive though it remains, indicates that older chaplains tend to give excessive questionnaire length and lack of time as their primary reasons for failure to return questionnaires.

It is not, of course, this age bias per se that is so worrisome; we must also be aware that there *could* be other variables (whose bias we cannot test) that differ significantly between my chaplain population and the sample of it represented in the returned questionnaires. Nevertheless, since neither denomination nor rank showed significant effects on return-rates, it is at least possible that the slight age bias is not directly related to any of my study's more important variables.

NOTES

1. Two works rate a partial exemption from this criticism. First there is a master's thesis by Chaplain (Col.) Clifford E. Keys, Jr., U.S.A., which is aimed at researching a specific problem of particular interest to the Chaplain Corps; there was no reason for Chaplain Keys to concern himself with broader issues. (See *Student Research Project 86*). In another work (a dissertation by Chaplain Alexander B. Aronis) there is some attempt to compare opinions of chaplains and commanding officers. (See *A Comparative Study of the Opinion of Navy Chaplains and Their Commanding Officers On Role Expectations, Deficiencies, and Preferred In-Service Education for Navy Chaplains.*) These and other studies of the chaplaincy are briefly reviewed in a later chapter.

2. Each civilian denomination supplying chaplains (and their number is legion—at least 40 to 45; it varies) must have an agency or agent that endorses members of its ordained clergy to the military services. No clergyman can be commissioned chaplain without such endorsement, nor can the military services maintain a clergyman as chaplain if the civilian denomination withdraws its endorsement of him.

3. Further discussions of denominational differences appear in a later chapter.

4. Here there was a small problem, for the chaplains' roster was not always precise in its description of any given chaplain's denomination. For example, a few chaplains from the Lutheran Missouri Synod were listed as LUTH instead of LUTH (M.S.); they received questionnaires despite my original intention to exclude the Missouri Synod. Similarly, United Methodist chaplains were marked either UMETH or METH. The overwhelming majority of METH chaplains are United Methodist, but a few are from Methodist splinter groups. A similar situation occurred with respect to the Southern Baptists. If any chaplains from the smaller denominations slipped into my sample returns (and I am reasonably sure at least three did), they were simply classified and analyzed with the major denominations.

5. This included almost every army unit to which a chaplain of any denomination was assigned. It also included one joint-service unit commanded by an air force officer. If a unit was commanded by a general officer, the questionnaire was addressed to "Commanding General, Attention: Personnel Officer."

6. For the Lutherans, the sample was drawn from the "Clerical Roster" in the *1972 Yearbook, Lutheran Church in America*. Sampling was done with replacement, and the names of two clergymen appeared twice; their responses were consequently double-weighted. For the Catholics, *The Official Catholic Directory, Anno Domini 1972* was used. The sample was taken from the list of Regular and Secular Clergy. The Baptist sample was drawn from the *Annual of the Southern Baptist Convention, Nineteen Hundred and Seventy One*. (Included in my sample was one American Baptist minister serving a Southern Baptist parish in Georgia.) For the Methodists, I drew my sample from full-connection ministers listed in the *General Minutes of the Annual Conference of the United Methodist Church*.

7. Strictly speaking, the term "sample" should be applied only to the set of civilian clergymen to whom I sent questionnaires. In the case of the chaplains and of the commanding officers, I made every attempt to exhaust the populations. Still, for convenience, I often say "sample" in reference to any or all of the three groups.

8. I did not wish my pilot questionnaire to "alert" chaplains from the denominations to be included in the major survey. (At the time I did not intend to include the Lutherans in my major survey.) I assumed that the chaplains of these denominations would be sufficiently similar to my target denominations to be of assistance in designing the final survey instrument.

9. In the case of chaplains, the code numbers had an additional function. They were keyed to my "chaplain roster," which included not only addresses but also ages, ranks, and components for all active-duty chaplains. I was thus able to omit such questions from my chaplain questionnaire, which was much too long at

any rate. Thus code numbers were affixed to first- *and* second-mailing chaplain questionnaires but only to first-mailing questionnaires for military commanders and civilian clergymen.

10. For both outgoing and return postage, surface mail was utilized within the continental United States, and airmail was utilized for chaplains and military officers assigned to units with APOs.

11. There is a good reason for this extremely high second mailing return rate. A number of units would have changed commanders in the two months between my first and second mailings. These new commanders could be expected to return these second mailing questionnaires at a "first-mailing" rate.

12. Roy E. Licklider, *The Private Nuclear Strategists,* p. 13.

13. James N. Rosenau, *National Leadership and Foreign Policy,* p. 49, note.

14. An artilleryman.

15. A Lutheran pastor, 47 years old. Note: In citing quotations from questionnaires I have *occasionally* falsified deliberately the age, rank, or denomination of the respondent. Furthermore, records of code numbers and quotation sources have been destroyed. Thus it is not possible for anyone to attribute with absolute certainty any quotation to any particular individual. For civilian clergymen, age and denomination are cited; for military commanders, rank and branch are cited; for chaplains, denomination and rank are cited. Finally, I was pleased to note that most of the comments I received concerning my survey were highly complimentary; the critical responses reproduced previously are atypical.

16. A Methodist captain.

17. A Methodist major.

18. A Catholic captain. (I have never been in Quang Tri Province.)

19. A Southern Baptist lieutenant colonel.

20. A Catholic major.

21. This is not the place to discuss the business of hypothesis testing in probit analysis. Good references are D. J. Finney, *Probit Analysis,* or a chapter in Goldberger's *Econometric Theory.* Briefly, the significance of a probit coefficient is tested by an examination of the log of the likelihood ratio (which, after a couple of transformations, is distributed as a χ^2 variable with degrees of freedom equal to the number of constraints put on the data). In the multivariate probit described here, the coefficient of D is associated with a probability greater than .25; the coefficient of G is associated with a probability greater than .50; the effects of D and G taken together are associated with a probability greater than .25. Statisticians will be quick to note that the purposes of the present analysis are only descriptive; we are not currently interested in making inferences about a larger hypothetical population of returners/nonreturners. Therefore, tests of "significance" do not have their usual meaning relative to a larger population. Instead, I have used them as an indicator of which relationships are sufficiently "improbable" to be interesting. For a sophisticated rationale for such use of "significance" tests, see J. Johnston, *Econometric Methods,* Ch. 1.

22. Lest I be accused of oversimplification, let me state that there is an important difference from regression in that the probit coefficients are calculated not by a least squares matrix algebra method but by an iterative method of maximum likelihood estimation. Thus they should be distinguished by some notation from the familiar least squares regression coefficients.

23. Each age was calculated as a whole number of years, rounding down, as of 31 January 1972. Thus a chaplain's age was calculated as follows: age = 1972 – birthyear.
24. "Active Duty Chaplain Roster," 1 October 1972.
25. Licklider, p. 207.

Chapter 4

THE CLAIMS OF CAESAR AND GOD:

DIFFERENTIATING THE ROLE EXPECTATIONS AND

VALUES OF CIVILIAN CLERGYMEN FROM THOSE

OF MILITARY COMMANDERS

The old captain was squatted on his heels, sipping coffee from a C-ration can. "Look here, Lieutenant," he said, "there's something you've got to learn right now. This army is a big machine, designed and built to grind down the enemy. Every man—without exception—must work to keep that machine running smooth. If you're not a drop of oil that lubricates, then you're a grain of sand, grating against the gears."

Gordon Zahn has written what is probably the very best published work on the military chaplaincy.[1] However, the chaplains to whom I've mentioned the subject are not too fond of the book. I suppose their attitude can be explained in part by the nature of Zahn's findings, which are not terribly complimentary toward the chaplaincy. Yet I do not think it entirely fair to blame all the disagreement on the chaplains' "resentful" natures; rather, there seems to be one basic flaw in Zahn's book. *The Military Chaplaincy* begins with two basic hypotheses: (1) role tension (clergyman vs. military officer) exists, and (2) such tension is generally resolved in favor of the military role dimension.[2] The second hypothesis is Zahn's main interest, and he attacks it with creative vigor. The second hypothesis should rest squarely on the first, however, and Zahn has not built his case any too carefully. As a social scientist, he never convincingly shows any conflict between the roles of clergyman and military officer; instead, he "proves" such conflict by references to his personal (basically pacifistic) theology.[3] For example, Zahn holds that the fire-bombing of Dresden was absolutely incompatible with Christian ethics. He therefore "finds" that any chaplain who would not oppose such an action has resolved role tension in favor of the military role dimension.

The problems surrounding such an approach soon become obvious. We must question from the very beginning the author's theological analysis. However appealing we may find the idea of rules in war, we must not proclaim it as a part of general Christian doctrine. Protestant theologians (pacifists and nonpacifists alike from Luther on) have been especially prone to reject the notion of limits to combat. For example, Karl Barth, probably the most influential theologian of this century, wished to reject any form of war under all but the most extreme of conditions; only God himself could legitimately command a man to engage in battle. Yet Barth was quick to say that once war had broken out, the killing was not to be limited, either in extent or in mode of application.[4] In Roman Catholic theology Zahn is on somewhat safer ground, but even the most extreme official condemnation of population bombing has its escape clauses.[5]

Though doctrine has always left at least some room for individual Christians to make their own decisions about the limits of war, each of the major churches has usually maintained some official position, however broad or unspecific. The basic Catholic view of war is stated by Thomas Aquinas in Question 40 of the *Summa*.[6] A Christian citizen should be prepared to participate in wars declared by his sovereign, but the Christian sovereign is allowed to wage only just wars.[7] The justice of a war is to be judged according to three criteria. First, it must be declared by a legal political sovereign. Second, the cause for which the war is fought must be basically righteous ("those who are attacked should be attacked because they deserve it . . ."). Third, the belligerents must believe that the evil that would result from not fighting the war would be greater than the evil caused by the exigencies of combat.[8] Furthermore, once the war has commenced, "there are certain rights of war and covenants, which ought to be observed even among enemies."[9]

Under no conditions should a priest be enrolled as a soldier because (1) he who kills (even in a just war) should not administer the sacraments and (2) the unrestful nature of military pursuits hinders the contemplation of God.[10] Nevertheless, since the Christians involved in war are in (especial) need of the sacraments, "prelates and clerics may, by the authority of their superiors, take part in wars, not indeed by taking up arms themselves, but by affording spiritual help to those who fight justly, by exhorting and absolving them, and by other spiritual helps."[11]

Organizationally, the Catholic chaplain is under quite well-defined ties to his denomination. The priest who is endorsed to be a chaplain (and subsequently commissioned as such) is transferred from the authority of his diocese to that of the Military Ordinate. The Military Ordinate is a dioceselike structure under the vicarage of the Archbishop of New York, and the chaplain priest is subject to the discipline of that bishop.

Whereas Catholics take their denominational views on war from Aquinas, Lutherans derive theirs from the writings of Martin Luther. For Luther, the sinful condition of mankind meant that temporal government was a necessity: By use of the sword, a temporal government was able to check some of the outward manifestations of evil; thus government was a gift of God's providence.[12] War became a legitimate political activity when it was undertaken with the aim of preserving God's gift of government. Christians should under no conditions participate in an "unjust" war (exactly what made a war "just" was never definitely explained by Luther; his follower Melanchthon brought in natural-law criteria, and the Lutheran "just war" came to resemble that of the Catholics).[13] In cases of doubt, however, it was morally safest for Lutherans to obey the secular authorities.[14] In any event, Luther insisted that the pastor should bring the good news of salvation by grace to all men everywhere, in or out of military service,[15] and this belief provided the basic justification for a Lutheran chaplaincy.

It is difficult to delineate any general Baptist position on questions of church and state, for the Baptist ecclesiastical "structure" is really defined in terms of radically independent congregations. Furthermore, even within those congregations great emphasis is placed on the free, God-guided conscience of the individual members.[16] Thus as Sanders says, "The Baptists' emphasis on individualism causes them to see the nature of church and state in terms of the individual and the state."[17] The same attitude is applied to the problem of war. Historically, Baptists have sometimes been a peace church, but now their attitudes cover the whole spectrum. The Southern Baptists are often classified as staunch political conservatives, but even this is a dangerous generalization. The Southern Baptist chaplain can be expected to have loose organizational (though perhaps very high affectational) ties to his denomination. His relationship to his military congregation will not be strictly defined by any dictates from his denomination.

The basic Methodist view of war is very negative: "The Church believes that war and bloodshed are contrary to the Christian conception of human welfare and violate the basic principles of universal brotherhood, and therefore are not compatible with the gospel and the spirit of Christ."[18]

Nevertheless, the church makes no definitive statement on the morality of individual participation in war, for this would interfere with the immediate contact of God with the individual conscience, which the Methodists (like the Baptists) are most anxious to affirm. The *Discipline*'s statement on war and peace continues: "God alone is the Lord of the conscience. Therefore, the Church recognizes the right of the individual member to answer the call of his government according to the dictates of his conscience and his sense of duty."[19]

In theory the United Methodist chaplain is under the close and immediate supervision of his church. He remains a member of his local annual conference; he is still subject to the ecclesiastical authority of that conference's bishop, who can (at least according to doctrine) assign him to any conference parish he (the bishop) may choose. Furthermore, since the chaplain generally serves far outside the geographical bounds of his home conference, he also relates to the church through the Commission on Chaplains and Related Ministries, a supraconference body with headquarters in Washington, D.C. The Methodist Church expects her chaplains to be many things; among the most important are:

> A minister in good standing in his annual conference, ready as are other ministers to move into differing situations, to be adaptable without necessarily conforming.

> * * *

> A minister with dual allegiance—to his church and to the institution within which he works—but whose ministry could not continue without his Church's endorsement and support.

> * * *

> ... one whose task is to keep alive the Christian interpretation of life—within another system.[20]

Like the religious denominations, the United States Army has certain doctrinal ideas of what a chaplain should be. As we have seen, regulations assign to the unit commander final responsibility for everything concerning his unit and the welfare of its personnel. To assist and advise the commander with matters (generally "technical") of which he has only limited competence, there exist special staff officers. One such special staff member is the medical officer or surgeon; another is the chaplain:

> The commander is responsible for the religious life, morals, and morale of the command (AR165-15). The chaplain is a member of the special staff and acts as advisor and consultant to the commander in all matters related to religion, morals, and morale as affected by religion in the command. The chaplain assists the commander and his staff to integrate the principles of good moral conduct and citizenship into the training program and the total life of the command (AR600-30).[21]

Within this advisory role the chaplain is saddled with a few duties that could be of direct military importance.[22] Perhaps the most important is the area of citizenship[23] and morale: "The chaplain will stimulate and guide the growth of the spiritual and moral sense of obligation to enable the soldier to be a faithful citizen and a devoted defender of the nation."[24] In addition, "From the time the young soldier enters the Army, it is the responsibility of the chaplain to make every effort to assist the soldier to render a creditable service to the Army."[25]

The army further states that the chaplain may have the additional role of advising his commander about the religion of the population indigenous to the theater of operations: "The field army chaplain should be prepared to advise the appropriate staff officers of the impact of comparative religions on psychological warfare operations."[26] Moreover, "[the Special Forces Group Chaplain] should be prepared to advise and assist the commander in the considerations of indigenous religions as they affect unconventional warfare and counterinsurgency plans, training, and operations."[27]

Though these quasi-military functions may be of some importance to the military service, the army certainly does not put any great stress upon them. Overall, the position of the chaplain is described like this: "Though he is a commissioned officer and wears the uniform of the U.S. Army, he is, first of all, minister, priest, or rabbi. The Army officially describes a chaplain's duties as 'analogous to those performed by clergymen in civilian life.' "[28]

The organizational position of the chaplain is, of course, quite clearly defined. Chaplains are assigned to all army installations and to all units capable of extended unsupported operations.[29] A chaplain is subject to the chain of command beginning with his unit commander (who is responsible for completing the chaplain's officer-efficiency reports). In addition, he is under the supervisory control of the chaplain of the next higher military unit. The chaplain is commissioned (as are all officers) by direction of the president; however, he can be retained as a chaplain only as long as he has the endorsement of his (civilian) denomination. Chaplains normally begin their service as captains; they can be promoted up through the rank of brigadier general (Deputy Chief of Chaplains) to major general (Chief of Chaplains). Most active-duty chaplains have reserve commissions, though a few come onto active duty through the National Guard (and are commissioned NGUS). Regular Army commissions are not at all uncommon: "Regular Army commissions are usually offered those chaplains on full-time active duty who have been tried and proven, showing special aptitudes, competency, and efficiency in their Army service."[30]

The chaplain's rank does not automatically entitle him to command authority; the chaplain (whatever his grade) is not generally authorized to give a lawful order. The title of address (regardless of rank) is simply *Chaplain*. In official correspondence, the rank is given in parentheses: "Chaplain (LTC) John Q. Smith."

The purpose of this chapter is to explain what the civilian denominations and the army want chaplains to do and be. Thus far we can say at least this much: The official and doctrinal definitions give the chaplains a lot of running room! Now let us turn to the definitions of application, as given by civilian clergymen and military commanders.

One important item[31] on each of my questionnaires sought to gain information about various chaplain functions:

14. Today's chaplain is called upon to perform a specialized ministry which includes many important tasks. Below I have listed eleven functions which various chaplains have seen as very important. Please mark the item *you* feel is most important with a "1", the second-most important item with a "2", and so on. Please mark all items. If you feel that any item describes a function *not* appropriate for a chaplain, please mark it with an "X". Please order the functions as you would in a combat situation.

____ The chaplain helps men gain the spiritual strength that will enable them to perform their duties more effectively despite the suffering and hardships of military operations.

____ The chaplain is concerned with evangelism and conversion.

____ The chaplain helps to bolster the troops' fighting spirit and morale.

____ The chaplain counsels troops on personal problems.

____ The chaplain preaches a message of reconciliation, emphasizing that even the enemy must not be hated.

____ The chaplain helps troops make the difficult personal adjustments required by extended operations in a hostile environment.

The Claims of Caesar and God

___ The chaplain prays that God will grant victory.

___ The chaplain administers the sacraments and conducts worship services.

___ The chaplain visits with and ministers to the sick and wounded.

___ The chaplain acts as a special staff officer advising the commanding officer.

___ The chaplain stresses that obedience to the properly constituted authorities is a Christian duty.

These 11 categories are divisible into two groups. On the one hand there are chaplain tasks clearly analogous to the duties any civilian clergyman might be expected to perform—namely, the second, fourth, eighth, and ninth options. On the other hand there are chaplain tasks that should be especially relevant to a military environment. Into this class I put the first, third, sixth, seventh, tenth, and eleventh options.

Table 4.1 presents mean scores, by sample group, for all the options. Since the items were rated in order of importance from "1" ("most important") to "11" ("least important"),[32] the lower mean scores indicate a greater degree of importance for options so rated. With both the clergymen and the commanders, two rating numbers are given for each task option. The first number (e.g., 3.62) is the mean of all ratings given the task option by all members of the group designated at the column head. The second number (an integer in parentheses) shows the

Table 4.1: Comparison of Clergymen's and Commanders' Ratings for 11 Chaplain Task Options

Ratings Given by:		Task Option Rated
Clergymen	Commanders	
3.62 (1)	4.3 (4)	The chaplain visits with and ministers to the sick and wounded.
3.63 (2)	4.4 (5)	The chaplain administers the sacraments and conducts worship services.
3.9 (3)	4.1 (3)	The chaplain counsels troops on personal problems.
4.5 (4)*	3.1 (1)*	*The chaplain helps men gain the spiritual strength that will enable them to perform their duties more effecitvely despite the suffering and hardships of military operations.
4.6 (5)	12.6 (10)	The chaplian preaches a message of reconciliation, emphasizing that even the enemy must not be hated.

4.9	(6)*	3.8	(2)*	*The chaplain helps troops make the difficult personal adjustments required by extended operations in a hostile environment.
6.5	(7)	12.8	(11)	The chaplain is concerned with evangelism and conversation.
10.6	(8)*	5.6	(6)*	*The chaplain acts as a special staff officer advising the commanding officer.
11.9	(9)*	11.4	(8)*	*The chaplain stresses that obedience to the properly constituted authorities is a Christian duty.
12.3	(10)*	6.1	(7)*	*The chaplain helps to bolster the troops' fighting spirit and morale.
14.8	(11)*	12.5	(9)*	*The chaplain prays that God will grant victory.

option's overall rank for the column head group; (1) indicates "most important;" (11) indicates "least important," and so on. The "military functions" and their ratings are marked with an asterisk.

Table 4.1 confirms, as we had hypothesized, that commanders accorded the military functions (marked with an asterisk) more importance than did the clergymen. For every one of those six tasks, the mean score for the military officers was lower (indicating greater importance) than the corresponding score for civilian clergymen. In regard to five of the six functions, the difference in means was significant well beyond the .05 level.[33] Similarly, the converse of this relationship is also true; for each of the five "regular clergyman" tasks, the score of the civilian clergymen is lower (indicating greater importance) than that of the military commanders. This clear substantiation of our first hypothesis demonstrates that a more detailed examination of chaplain tasks is appropriate.

Several of the options are readily dispensed with. Clergymen and commanders are agreed that praying for victory is not an important task. (Mean scores are 14.8 for the clergymen and 12.5 for the commanders.) Similarly, neither group places much stress on the legitimation-of-obediency option. ("Obedience to the properly constituted authorities is a Christian duty." Civilian clergymen rate it ninth with a score of 11.9; military commanders place it eighth with 11.4.) Clergymen think it's improper, and commanders don't think it should be necessary. As one veteran infantry officer put it, if a commander can't instill obedience and discipline in his own troops, there's precious little a chaplain can do to help.[34]

On the "pastoral" functions there is little difference between the ratings of the clergymen and of the commanders. The clergymen rate the visitation of the sick first, and though the commanders rate it fourth, there is no statistically significant difference in the scores (3.6 and 4.3, respectively). In addition, marginal comments show that both groups hold this function to be very important. Both the clergymen and the commanders rate counseling tasks third (3.9 and 4.1, respectively). Similarly, the priestly function of the chaplain is thought by both groups to be quite appropriate, but the clergymen rate it as significantly more important than do the commanders.

On the matter of the chaplain as a member of the commander's staff, the ratings of the clergymen and officers are very different (the clergymen rate it eighth with 10.6, the commanders rate it sixth with 5.6). Nevertheless, I do not think we should make too much of this difference. Responses to other questions indicate that civilian clergymen do in fact want the chaplain to advise his commanding officer in the fields of morals and religion—and this is precisely his staff job. Military commanders, on the other hand, do not generally seek much specific staff advice from the chaplain, but since the military manuals state that he is a special staff officer, that function must be of some importance.

Up to this point the task evaluations of clergymen and commanders have been remarkably similar. Two chaplain task areas, however, remain to be discussed: "prophetic" tasks[35] and "legitimation-of-suffering" tasks.[36] Clergymen and commanders disagree greatly over the importance of the chaplain's prophetic ministry. The former rate the evangelism-and-conversion option seventh (score of 6.5), and the latter rate it last (score of 12.8). Apparently the military commanders believe that a combat chaplain has enough to do without recruiting new members for the church. An even greater disparity of views exists concerning the reconciliation option (quoted again in note 35). Civilian clergymen evaluate the option as quite important (fifth, with a score of 4.6), but military commanders rate it next to last (tenth, with a score of 12.6—not significantly different from the commanders' bottom-ranked task). One marginal comment was revealing. An officer had simply marked through the option, scratching it out; he included only the terse observation, "B.S."[37] While chaplains may not always be expected to help the military, they are certainly not supposed to hinder it.

There are also ways the chaplain may be able to help the commander. These are expressed in our legitimation-of-suffering options. If the military commanders desire to adapt religion to serve a legitimating function, we can expect them to rate these three items as more important than will the civilian clergymen. This is indeed the case. The commanders rate the "spiritual strength" option first (3.1); the clergymen rate it fourth (4.5). The commanders rate the "fighting spirit and morale" seventh (6.1), and the clergymen place it next to last (tenth, score of 12.3). The "personal adjustment" option is rated second by commanders (3.8) and sixth (4.9) by the clergymen. The differences in these mean ratings are statistically significant at a very high level.

Commanding officers, then, are willing to use religion to legitimate military service. Yet this legitimating is indirect and quite probably unconscious. The commanders reject rather soundly crude, direct legitimation implied by the chaplain-stresses-obedience option. They appear to prefer the more subtle function emphasized by Marx: The chaplain (thereby religion) gives the soldier spiritual strength to endure the hardships of military life. As one colonel added at the end of the questionnaire, "To me it boils down to the chaplain helping sustain courage—personal and unit."[38] Since the American cause is held to be just, the chaplain is expected to help give men the courage they need to carry on the battle for the right. How can we blame the colonel? He might, after all, have been quoting Luther: "And if the heart is bold and courageous, the fist is more powerful, a man and even his horse are more energetic, everything turns out better, and every happening and deed contributes to the victory which God then gives."[39]

On their list of chaplain duties, then, the commanders generally rate legitimating tasks quite high, and a great deal higher than do the civilian clergymen. The officers' ratings, however, are not all the same, and I sought to determine the origin of the variance. Numerous background variables were examined—age, rank, branch, religious affiliation, number of decorations—but (as I had suspected) none was significantly correlated with commanders' ratings of legitimating tasks. There remained, however, one variable that was of more theoretical interest. In one item on the questionnaire for military officers I sought to determine the relative importance of chaplains to the military commanders.[40]

17. If you were the commanding officer of an infantry battalion, in what order of importance would you rate the following personnel, who might be in or attached to your unit? (Mark the most important with a "1", the second-most important with a "2", and so on. To be more specific, let me suggest that the battalion is in a garrison situation but may be called into combat at very short notice; let me suggest, in fact, that the battalion under consideration is one from the 82 Airborne Division.)

___ S-1
___ Chaplain
___ Assistant S-3
___ Medical Officer
___ Maintenance Officer
___ Sergeant-Major

It seemed to me that if religious legitimation (through the chaplain) were desired by the military, the commanders who rated legitimating tasks as highly appropriate would also tend to see chaplains as relatively more important; thus we can derive the following hypothesis:

Hypothesis: Among military commanders, high ratings for legitimating tasks will be positively correlated with high importance ratings for chaplains.

Table 4.2 summarizes my findings in this area. The "mean legitimacy score" is the mean for all the three legitimation-of-suffering tasks ("spiritual strength," "fighting spirit and morale," and "personal adjustments"; remember, lower scores indicate *more* emphasis on legitimating tasks). The "importance" rating is the number 2 through 6 (no commander rated the chaplain as 1, most important) with which a commander marked the option "chaplain" in question 17. The direction of the relationship is obviously that predicted by our hypothesis.[41]

Table 4.2: Importance of Chaplains as Rated by Commanders[a]

	2 (very important)	3	4	5	6 (relatively unimportant)
Mean legitimacy score	3.0	4.0	3.9	4.7	4.8

[a] Commanders who think chaplains are important also think legitimation is an important chaplain function.

One further item touched on the matter of religious legitimation. In the second part of this question (item 25 for the civilian clergymen and item 26 for the military commanders); the clergymen and commanders were asked to state what they thought a chaplain should do if approached by a soldier seeking to become a conscientious objector.

25. Imagine this situation, which could confront the chaplain of a combat infantry unit. One day, after the unit has returned to a relatively secure base camp, a soldier goes to the chaplain and says that he believes God does not wish for him to participate further in the war. The soldier expresses his desire to become a conscientious objector. What do you believe the average chaplain *will* do?

What do you feel the chaplain *should* do? _____

The answers were coded from "1," very promilitary ("kick the soldier out and get him back into the line," etc.), to "5," quite antimilitary ("praise him for following his conscience and get him out of the army no matter what"). The difference in the mean ratings of clergymen and commanders was not very great, but it was certainly in the direction that would be predicted by a legitimation hypothesis[42] (commanders, 3.16; clergymen 3.62); the clergymen are slightly more ready to help a soldier achieve conscientious objector (CO) status. In general the clergymen gave an answer like, "Get at the heart of the matter. If [the soldier is] a true conscientious objector; help him achieve status."[43] The commanders usually said something like, "Counsel to determine sincerity and follow the regulations." [The "regulations" (Section 2-12 of AR 600-200 for enlisted men, Section III-10 of AR 614-260 for officers) require that the soldier be counseled by the chaplain, who will make a recommendation, based his perception of the individual's sincerity, to the commanding officer. The CO applicant is placed on noncombatant status pending a higher level decision on his request.] Most commanders see the regulations on conscientious objection as proper and just (though a few would have the chaplain convince a CO applicant to return to combat duty). After all, the individual objector will be quickly replaced, presumably with a less reluctant combat· soldier. What apparently concerns many commanders is the possibility of "conscientious" objection spreading to other members of the unit who are motivated less by a sense of religious conviction than by the desire to avoid combat duty. Thus the commanders insist (as do the regulations) that their chaplains probe deeply to determine an applicant's sincerity. In general the commanders believe that the road to conscientious objection should be kept open[44] but that it must never become too smooth!

One additional question was asked about the relationship of a chaplain's role to military efficiency.

Civilian clergymen:

15. While a good chaplain's work is often helpful to the Army, there *may* be occasional instances in which a chaplain feels compelled by his religious convictions to do or say something that could prove detrimental to the efficient conduct of military operations. Would you think that the average chaplain, at some time in his career, has been faced with such a situation?

Military commanders:

15. While a good chaplain's work is often helpful to the Army, there *may* be occasional instances in which a chaplain feels compelled by his religious convictions to do or say something that could prove detrimental to the efficient conduct of military operations. Are you aware of any such instances that have actually occurred? _____

The Claims of Caesar and God

Table 4.3: Extent of Chaplain-Army Conflict Expected by Clergymen and Commanders

Respondents	Do situations arise in which chaplains feel morally bound to oppose military activities?	
	Yes or Probably Yes (%)	No or Probably No (%)
Military commanders	10	90
Civilian clergymen	95	5

Table 4.3 gives the distribution of answers. The implication is quite clear; the civilian clergymen expect chaplains to be in a role of conflict within the army; the military commanders have not seen this to be the case.

ATTITUDES AND QUALITIES[45]

Thus far we have been concerned about the tasks a chaplain is expected to perform by civilian clergymen and military commanders. We have discovered that despite a great deal of similarity between the ratings of the clergymen and commanders, there are also some important differences. Eventually we shall be interested in determining where between these two poles the chaplains lie. Do they define their tasks more nearly like the clergymen or the commanders? This question of similarity, however, may be asked on a much wider front. Every army chaplain is both an ordained clergyman and a commissioned officer. Therefore it makes sense to ask in specific areas whether the chaplain's image of himself is more nearly that of an officer or a clergyman. This question is the subject of the next chapter.

Now, however, we inquire, *What are these military and clerical self-definitions?* We shall examine this question in two areas: (1) attitudes toward certain issues, and (2) evaluation of certain personal qualities and beliefs.

Items 19 through 23 on the questionnaire for military officers sought to examine issue-oriented attitudes.[46]

19. Overall, do you feel yourself more nearly oriented toward the values of nationalism or toward those of a united world?

NATIONALISM				UNITED WORLD
1	2	3	4	5

20. Do you tend to agree or disagree with the following statement? "In international relations, the interests of the United States should always come first."

AGREE   DISAGREE

1   2   3   4   5

21. Do you agree or disagree with the following statement? "An insult to your honor should not be forgotten."

AGREE   DISAGREE

1   2   3   4   5

22. Do you think that you should remain very sensitive to human suffering, or do you feel you have to steel yourself to some extent so that you will be better able to carry out your duties in the face of such suffering?

REMAIN VERY   STEEL MYSELF
SENSITIVE   SOMEWHAT

1   2   3   4   5

23. Do you feel it would be morally right to bomb (with nuclear weapons) the civilian population centers of an enemy nation in retaliation for similar attacks on our own population centers?

MORALLY RIGHT   MORALLY WRONG
TO BOMB   TO BOMB

1   2   3   4   5

The responses to these questions were coded according to the number circled. Coding transformations were made so that the *expected* clergyman response was for all questions a smaller number than the *expected* commander response.[47] (Questions 19, 20, 21, and 23 were so transformed.) Mean scores are presented in Table 4.4. In each case the mean for the civilian clergymen is significantly lower ($p < .01$) than that for the military commanders, though clearly the differences are far from extreme.[48]

EVALUATION OF PERSONAL QUALITIES AND BELIEFS

Besides their differences in attitudes, I also expected civilian priests and ministers to differ from army officers in evaluating certain personal qualities and beliefs. Item 25 on the questionnaire for military officers[49] sought to elicit such an evaluation.

Table 4.4: Comparison of Clergymen's and Commanders' Ratings of Scaled, Issue-Oriented Items

Respondents	Question 19: Nationalism or united world? (Higher scores indicate pro-nationalism.)	Question 20: Should U.S. interests always come first? (Higher scores indicate yes.)	Question 21: Should insult to honor be forgotten? (Higher scores indicate no.)	Question 22: Remain sensitive or steel oneself? (Higher scores indicate "steel oneself")	Question 23: Is it morally wrong to bomb? (Higher scores indicate not wrong to bomb.)	Total Score
Civilian clergymen	2.26	2.09	1.62	2.18	1.93	10.08
Military commanders	3.62	3.74	2.73	3.32	3.85	17.26

[79]

25. It probably requires a very special sort of person to fulfill effectively the challenges of the military profession. Below I have listed fourteen descriptive phrases. Some of them are appropriate for describing a professional military officer; others are inappropriate. Some may be neutral. In the spaces provided, please mark with a "1" the quality you feel is most important for a military officer to possess. Mark the second-most important with a "2", and so on. Please mark all items.

___ boastful
___ strict
___ willing to forgive an offender again and again
___ willing to use violence to obtain justice
___ kind
___ feels killing in war is justified
___ believes in God as the final authority and absolute ruler over all men and nations
___ aggressive
___ meticulously avoids all "foul" or "improper" language
___ quick-tempered
___ unconditional in loyalty to the United States
___ loves enemies
___ gentle
___ dislikes involvement in any form of violence

Using the numbers with which you rated the above items, please tell which qualities you feel would be a positive help to the military officer, which you feel would be neutral, and which you feel would be detrimental:

___ I believe that the qualities I marked with numbers *1* through___ would be helpful; those I marked with numbers___ through___ would be neutral; those I marked with numbers___ through *14* would be detrimental.

The four following qualities were rated very nearly the same by the clergymen and commanders: "boastful," "kind," "meticulously avoids all 'foul' or 'improper' language," and "quick-tempered." Let us remember that all four were rated about the same, then temporarily set them aside and limit our tabular analysis to the remaining qualities (Tables 4.5 and 4.6). In each table the mean score is the mean of all ratings given the corresponding quality by all members of the group concerned; "Rating" indicates the overall rank of the corresponding quality for the group in question.

The differences in the ratings given by the two professions are almost shocking, at least at first glance. It would appear that no one could possibly feel at once like a military officer and like a clergyman. Yet perhaps the differences are not really as great as they appear. We recall the four qualities noted earlier that were rated alike by both professions. Next we note that the neutral-rated qualities allow room for shifting and interpretation. Then we can realize that there are only four (out of 14) qualities rated positively by one profession and negatively by another. These four qualities are "feels killing in war is justified" and "unconditional in loyalty to the United States" (both rated positively by the commanders and negatively by the clergymen) plus "willing to forgive an offender again and again" and "loves enemies" (both rated positively by the clergymen and negatively by the commanders). In our examination of the chaplains we shall pay particular attention to their ratings of these critical qualities.[50]

Table 4.5: Ratings of Qualities

General Rating	Quality	Rating	Mean Score
	by Civilian Clergymen		
"Positive"	God as final ruler	(1)	2.4
	Forgive again and again	(2)	3.6
	Gentle	(3)	4.0
	Loves enemies	(4)	4.2
"Neutral"	Dislikes involvement in violence	(5)	7.0
	Strict	(6)	8.0
	Aggressive	(7)	8.1
"Negative"	Loyalty to United States	(8)	10.4
	Violence to obtain justice	(9)	10.7
	Killing in war	(10)	10.8

Table 4.6: Ratings of Qualities

General Rating	Quality	Rating	Mean Score
	by Military Commanders		
"Positive"	Aggressive	(1)	2.8
	Loyalty to United States	(2)	2.9
	Strict	(3)	4.3
	Killing in war	(4)	5.7
	God as final ruler	(5)	5.9
"Neutral"	Violence to obtain justice	(6)	6.7
	Gentle	(7)	7.3
"Negative"	Forgive again and again	(8)	10.3
	Dislikes involvement in violence	(9)	11.0
	Loves enemies	(10)	11.6

SUMMARY

This chapter has shown, first of all, that the differences between clergymen and commanders are generally not extreme. Nevertheless, we have also seen that unit commanders believe a chaplain can and should help the army by making soldiers better able to withstand the hardships of military service: The chaplain is expected to "sustain courage." Civilian clergymen, on the other hand, do not generally believe such legitimation of suffering is an appropriate part of the chaplain's job. This contrast between the views of commanders and clergymen carries over into certain attitudes as well as the evaluation of some personal qualities and beliefs. These differences form a sort of continuum between the opinions of civilian clergymen and military officers. The next chapter attempts to determine where along this continuum the opinions of chaplains themselves fall.

NOTES

1. *The Military Chaplaincy: A Study of Role Tension in the Royal Air Force.*
2. Ibid., pp. 31-32.
3. Ibid., p. 18.
4. Karl Barth, *Church Dogmatics,* Vol. III/4, *The Doctrine of Creation,* pp. 453-454.
5. *Vatican II,* p. 294.
6. Aquinas, *Suhma Theologia,* Part II, Question 40, especially article 1.
7. In this chapter I present only the views of "just wars" that have traditionally been held as doctrine by the four denominations included in this research. However, the more general American view of "just wars" has been the subject of much recent discussion, and the popular view of what constitutes a just war appears to differ somewhat from doctrinal definitions.
8. Aquinas, Question 40, Article 1.
9. Ibid., Question 40, Article 3. See also *Vatican II,* p. 292.
10. Ibid., Question 40, Article 2.
11. Ibid., Question 40, Article 2.
12. Martin Luther, "Temporal Authority," in *Selected Writings,* Vol. 2, pp. 271-319.
13. Thomas G. Sanders, *Protestant Concepts of Church and State,* p. 48.
14. Most of Luther's discussion on war may be found in his *Whether Soldiers, too, Can Be Saved,* in *Selected Writings,* pp. 427-477.
15. Indeed, in his lengthy letter to professional soldier Assa von Luther Kram, Luther showed that it was proper for a pastor to lend encouragement to wavering soldiers. Thus their consciences would be clear and they could fight better! Ibid., see especially p. 432.
16. Sanders, pp. 199-200.
17. Ibid., p. 201-202.
18. *Book of the Discipline of the United Methodist Church,* p. 66.
19. Ibid., p. 66. It should be noted in passing that the Methodist Church also affirms the right of conscientious objection.

20. United Methodist Division of Interpretation, "What in the World is a Chaplain?"
21. U.S. Department of the Army, Field Manual 16-5, *The Chaplain*, p. 1.
22. It should be noted that the army (unlike the navy) forbids the unit commander to burden his chaplains with extra, nonreligious duties (athletics and recreation officer, charity fund drive officer, etc.).
23. Many critics of the chaplaincy focus their attacks on this role of citizenship/patriotism-building. I tend to agree with those critics, but admittedly my position is shaped in large part by my particular theological perspective.
24. Field Manual 16-5, p. 1.
25. Ibid., p. 6.
26. Ibid., p. 6.
27. Ibid., p. 52.
28. U.S. Department of the Army, Department of the Army Pamphlet 165-2, "The Challenge of the Chaplaincy in the United States Army."
29. This means, in practice, that chaplains are *assigned* down to the level of brigades or independent battalions. Frequently they are *attached* to a lower level. For example, chaplains assigned to an infantry brigade might be attached to battalions within that brigade.
30. Department of the Army Pamphlet 165-2.
31. This was question 14 on the questionnaires for civilian clergymen and military officers. It was question 25 on the chaplains' questionnaire. On all questionnaires the options to be rated were identical (except for a misspelling on the chaplains' questionnaire), and the introduction was changed only slightly (see Appendix). Here I have presented the item from the civilian clergymen's questionnaire.
32. A score of "20" was arbitrarily assigned as weight for any option(s) a respondent deemed entirely inappropriate (i.e., any he marked with an "X").
33. To say that such a relationship is significant at the .05 level is to say that the chances are overwhelming (greater than 95 in 100) that the relationship would not have shown up in our sample unless it also existed in the population from which the sample was taken.
34. A lieutenant colonel of infantry with 30 years' service.
35. Besides priestly and pastoral tasks, theologians speak of a clergyman's *prophetic duties* (e.g., the proclamation of the Gospel and the call to repentance, reconciliation, and salvation). Prophetic tasks were represented in my questionnaire by two options: "The Chaplain is concerned with evangelism and conversion," and "The Chaplain preaches a message of reconciliation, emphasizing that even the enemy must not be hated." Obviously these two task options no more than suggest the seriousness the chaplain's role of prophetic criticism might take on in wartime. The sensitivity of my sample groups precluded the inclusion of other, more penetrating options.
36. These include the task of maintaining morale, of making men better able to bear the suffering attendant to the life of a combat soldier. Such tasks were represented in my questionnaire by three options: "The Chaplain helps men gain the spiritual strength that will enable them to perform their duties more effectively despite the suffering and hardships of military operations"; "the chaplain helps to bolster the troops' fighting spirit and morale"; "the chaplain helps troops

make the difficult personal adjustments required by extensive operations in a hostile environment."

37. A captain of infantry. The reader should also recall the very "mildness" of the options I used to represent the chaplain's prophetic tasks. Even the clergymen might have torn up my questionnaires if I had worded the item more strongly.

38. A colonel of infantry.

39. Martin Luther, *Whether Soldiers, too, Can be Saved; Selected Writings*, p. 433.

40. The S-1 is the adjutant, who acts as a sort of personnel officer. The Assistant S-3 is the assistant to the operations officer (the S-3 himself is almost undoubtedly the most important member of a battalion commander's regular staff). The sergeant-major is the battalion's senior enlisted man.

41. The relationship is indeed statistically significant with $p < .01$. The strength of the relationship, however, is not at all large; the correlation coefficient of importance ratings with mean legitimacy scores *(R)* is .232.

42. The difference between the means is statistically significant at the level of $p < .001$. In all options for which coding involved more than the mere reporting of a number or a marked subresponse, checks were made for internal reliability. Intercoder reliability for all such options was quite high.

43. A 46-year-old United Methodist.

44. I must note for exception a certain colonel of infantry who replied that the chaplain would and should counsel, et cetera; the colonel went on to say, "Contrast these actions ... to what would happen in a really *good* professional army, such as the USSR, Israel, or Germany c. 1939!" [The emphasis is that of the colonel.]

45. Before passing even temporarily from the consideration of chaplain roles, I should note that the survey disclosed no convincing differences between how Methodist, Lutheran, Catholic, and Baptist clergymen define the proper tasks of a chaplain. (Intradenominational variability, however, was quite large.)

46. These items are from the questionnaire for military officers. The questionnaire for civilian clergymen included identically worded items (questions 17-21). My questionnaires also included two additional questions designed to measure issue-oriented attitudes, but respondents' marginal comments indicated serious ambiguities, and I therefore reluctantly removed those questions from all consideration.

47. The ends of the scale were simply switched. If a "1" were circled, the question was coded "5"; if a "2" were circled, the question was coded "4," and so on.

48. These attitudes again revealed few differences between denominations. Southern Baptists are slightly more nationalistic (score higher on questions 19 and 20); Lutherans and Roman Catholics are slightly more opposed to retaliation bombing (and see *Vatican II*, p. 294). The general picture remains one of great interdenominational similarity.

49. This was item 23 on the questionnaire for civilian clergymen. It was introduced as follows:

23. It probably requires a very special sort of person to fulfill effectively the challenges of the clergyman's vocation. Below I have listed fourteen descrip-

tive phrases. Some of them are appropriate for describing a clergyman; others are inappropriate. Some may be neutral. In the spaces provided, please mark with a "1" the quality you feel is most important for a clergyman to possess. Mark the second-most important with a "2", and so on. Please mark all items.

50. Once again the interdenominational differences are virtually negligible. The Southern Baptists are slightly more willing to forgive and love their enemies (more so especially than the Roman Catholics); they also give a slightly higher rating to loyalty to the United States (perhaps inconsistently, since they also rate belief in God's absolute lordship slightly higher than other denominations). I could discover no other large or interesting differences between denominations.

Chapter 5

"CHOOSE YOU THIS DAY....": WHICH ROLES AND VALUES THE CHAPLAINS ACTUALLY AFFIRM

[Joshua says to the assembled tribes of Israel,] Now therefore fear the LORD, and serve him in sincerity and in truth: and put away the gods which your fathers served on the other side of the flood, and in Egypt; and serve ye the LORD. And if it seem evil unto you to serve the LORD, choose you this day whom you will serve; whether the gods which your fathers served that were on the other side of the flood, or the gods of the Amorites, in whose land ye dwell: but as for me and my house, we will serve the LORD.

Joshua 24:14-15

In the previous chapter we saw how civilian clergymen would view the task of ministering to men in uniform. We also saw that military commanders would like to define that ministry somewhat differently. More specifically, they would like to reshape the religious ministry (as defined by the civilian denominations) to (1) emphasize the development of spiritual strength and courage in the face of adversity and suffering and (2) de-emphasize the prophetic call for repentance, forgiveness, and brotherhood. At least to that extent, they are asking for religious legitimation of military service. Thus the stage has been set for the present chapter. We know what the civilian denominations have "to offer"; we know what the military commanders would like "to buy." We shall now examine the final product presented by the chaplains, deferring the equally interesting question of "why?" until a later chapter.

If I were making a serious effort to learn whether chaplains legitimated the military, should I not at some point (preferably late in my questionnaire) throw subtlety to the winds and ask them bluntly? This I did in item 47:

[87]

47. Some of the military chaplaincy's more radical critics contend that the chaplaincy serves chiefly a legitimating function, that the presence in the Army of priests and ministers helps convince would-be pacifistic Christians that God really does approve of participation in military service and war. How would you answer such criticisms? (Note: If you tend to have a natural, violent reaction to this sort of criticism, please attempt to refrain from ripping up this questionnaire and tossing it into the trash can. You are so near the end!)____

I found it convenient to divide responses to this question into six different categories.

Class I (about 1.4%) included a small number of highly vocal chaplains who felt the army might be good enough to *deserve* religious legitimation; generally they stressed the army's civic action roles. I quote one answer at length:

> This question precisely illustrates a very common misunderstanding of the U.S. Armed Forces. The mission of the Army (at least, and I suspect this applies to the other armed services) is to keep the peace. There are literally thousands of instances where the U.S. Military has spent more time and energy in helping people than it has in the destruction of war. E.G.—the terrible hurricane that devastated the coast of the state of Mississippi several years ago—Army Engineer Battalions, Air Force units and other troops were the first (and probably stayed the longest) to come to the aid of that area. In severe weather the Armed Forces have spent thousands of dollars and many hours in rescue work—e.g., during a severe winter in Eastern Kentucky about 1966 a mountain lady in an isolated cabin began to have labor pains; the area was completely isolated by natural surroundings complicated by much snow, her husband struggled to a settlement, called someone else, who in turn finally got in touch with the Army at Fort Campbell, Kentucky, who immediately dispatched a doctor, a nurse, and several men in a helicopter and flew to the rescue. This has been done many times in other ways. The U.S. Forces gave thousands of dollars of food and equipment to Algeria in the 50's after devastating floods there; Panama has received Armed Forces aid literally hundreds of times when natural disasters struck, etc., etc. Certainly God does approve of participation in the military. Why not? Especially the U.S. Military. NOW, DON'T *YOU* TEAR UP THIS PAGE!!![1]

Class II (about 10.7%) chaplains were adamant in their denial of a legitimating function. Their most common answer was a firm "B.S." (not always euphemistically abbreviated). One respondent replied,

"Bull shit! Nothing is further from the truth. . . . I minister to individuals who are soldiers. I am not an institutional spokesman."[2]

Class III (about 6.6%) chaplains apparently held about the same views as those in class II but were a bit more moderate in expressing them.

Class IV included the majority (about 73.6%) of my respondents. These chaplains all felt that legitimation was an improper role and they wanted no part of it. Yet they saw as secondary if not irrelevant the question of whether they did in fact play that role simply (and necessarily) by virtue of their being clergymen in uniform. Christ's gospel, they believed, must be brought to all people. At present, the chaplaincy is the best instrument for bringing it to soldiers. Therefore, they are chaplains. Two replies are illustrative.

> Whenever the religious bodies are willing to supply pastors and priests not in uniform I'll gladly step down.[3]

> We are pastors and most will continue [to be so] after retirement from the Army. The only way I can provide a pastoral service to the paratrooper is to jump out of his stupid planes.[4]

Class V includes chaplains (about 5.3%) who are worried that in some way the army may be using them (or at least some of their colleagues) for legitimation: "Unfortunately, too many chaplains DO identify GOD and country. [However,] I think the critics are ill-informed as a rule."[5]

Class VI chaplains (2.2%) give similar opinions but express them less moderately:

> To a very high degree the chaplain is used as table dressing.[6]

> The criticism is essentially correct. Clergy who have gravitated to the chaplaincy are *often* of this political persuasion. Some are almost 'religious prostitutes' and have promotion and high salary constantly in mind.[7]

Thus answers to question 47 varied considerably. To simplify things, we should remember that more than 90% of the respondents held that the chaplain *does not* legitimate the military, and almost 99% felt that he *should not*. Asked straight out, chaplains want nothing to do with legitimation. Yet since we have defined legitimation in a rather roundabout way, we shall wish to examine data more directly comparable with the returns from the civilian clergymen and military commanders.

Item 25 on the questionnaire for military chaplains returns to the question of chaplain tasks.

25. Today's military chaplain has many important tasks to fulfill. Below I have listed eleven functions which various chaplains have seen as very important. Please mark the item *you* feel is most important with a "1", the second-most important item with a "2", and so on. Please mark all items. If you feel that any item describes a function *not* appropriate for a chaplain, please mark it with an "X". Please order the functions as you would in a combat situation.

____ The chaplain helps men gain the spiritual strength that will enable them to perform their duties more effectively despite the suffering and hardships of military operations.

____ The chaplain is concerned with evangelism and conversation.

____ The chaplain helps to bolster the troops' fighting spirit and morale.

____ The chaplain counsels troops on personal problems.

____ The chaplain preaches a message of reconciliation, emphasizing that even the enemy must not be hated.

____ The chaplain helps troops make the difficult personal adjustments required by extended operations in a hostile environment.

____ The chaplain prays that God will grant victory.

____ The chaplain administers the sacraments and conducts worship services.

____ The chaplain visits with and ministers to the sick and wounded.

____ The chaplain acts as a special staff officer advising the commanding officer.

____ The chaplain stresses that obedience to the properly constituted authorities is a Christian duty.

Table 5.1 presents the chaplains' mean evaluation for each of these task types. (Civilian clergymen's and commanders' evaluations are also given, from Table 4.1, for purposes of comparison.) A detailed analysis of this table reveals some differences between the ratings of the chaplains and those of the civilian clergymen. The former, for example, give slightly less weight than their civilian colleagues to the "prophetic" options, thus falling between the clergymen and the commanders.[8] Nevertheless, the similarity of the chaplain and civilian-clergyman ratings is most striking. However much these two groups may differ with respect to attitudes and the evaluation of beliefs and qualities (and it turns out that they differ slightly more in those areas), chaplains do define their ministry in essentially the same ways that civilian clergymen would wish; they are not greatly influenced by the desire of the commanders. This finding is further borne out by an examination of the question on conscientious objection (item 40 on the questionnaire for military chaplains).

40. Assume that you are serving as chaplain to a combat infantry unit. One day, after the unit has returned to a relatively secure base camp, a soldier comes to you and says that he believes God does not wish for him to participate further in the war. The soldier expresses his desire to become a conscientious objector. Briefly, what do you do?

Table 5.1: Comparison of Clergymen's, Chaplains', and Commanders' Ratings for 11 Chaplain Task Options[a]

Ratings Given by:			Task Option Rated
Clergymen	Chaplains	Commanders	
3.62 (1)	3.5 (2)	4.3 (4)	The chaplain visits with and ministers to the sick and wounded
3.63 (2)	2.6 (1)	4.4 (5)	The chaplain administers the sacraments and conducts worship services.
3.9 (3)	4.0 (3)	4.1 (3)	The chaplain counsels troops on personal problems.
4.5 (4)	4.9 (4)	3.1 (1)	The chaplain helps men gain the spiritual strength that will enable them to perform their duties more effectively despite the suffering and hardships of military operations.
4.6 (5)	5.9 (6)	12.6 (10)	The chaplain preaches a message of reconciliation, emphasizing that even the enemy must not be hated.
4.9 (6)	5.6 (5)	3.8 (2)	The chaplain helps troops make the difficult personal adjustments required by extended operations in a hostile environment.
6.5 (7)	7.9 (8)	12.8 (11)	The chaplain is concerned with evangelism and conversion.
10.6 (8)	7.1 (7)	5.6 (6)	The chaplain acts as a special staff officer advising the commanding officer.
11.9 (9)	12.7 (10)	11.4 (8)	The chaplain stresses that obedience to the properly constituted authorities is a Christian duty.
12.3 (10)	11.9 (9)	6.1 (7)	The chaplain helps to bolster the troops fighting spirit and morale.
14.8 (11)	15.2 (11)	12.5 (9)	The chaplain prays that God will grant victory.

With the clergymen, the chaplains, and the commanders, two rating numbers are given for each task-option. The first number [e.g., 3.62] is the mean of all ratings given the corresponding task option by all members of the group concerned. The second number [an integer presented in parentheses, e.g., (1)] shows the overall rank of the corresponding task option for the group concerned; (1) would indicate "most important"; (11) would indicate "least important," etc.

a. Ratings have significance described in connection with Table 4.1.

What do you think the unit commander would want you to do? _____

_____

Remember that the answers were coded from "1," very "promilitary" (the chaplain ought to "kick the soldier out and get him back into the line," etc.) to "5," quite "antimilitary" (the chaplain ought to "praise him for following his conscience and get him out of the army no matter what"). The mean coded response for commanders was 3.16; for civilian clergymen it was 3.62. Again the chaplains were much closer to the clergymen than to the commanders; their mean coded response was, in fact, 3.71, indicating that they might well take an even less "military" position on conscientious objection than the civilian clergymen would desire.

Does the chaplain believe it is his role to enhance the effectiveness of the fighting machine and thus contribute to the chances of obtaining victory? I had originally expected that such was the case; thus far, however, my data strongly indicate that it is not. This conclusion is further borne out by responses to the last item on the questionnaire for military chaplains.

48. Here is one last question before I let you get back to work. This one presents another imaginary situation — in fact, it is (to use a youth culture expression) "far out." Nevertheless, I do hope you'll answer it, for I'd really like to use it in my analysis. Many chaplains feel that they minister to soldiers as people, without taking into consideration the political justice of the cause for which they may be fighting. Suppose you found out that there were, in the army of another nation, a number of Christians who badly needed the service of a minister or priest (who could not be found among the citizens of their own country). If you were not in the US Army, would you feel you could serve those men as a chaplain

____ with the British Army?
____ with the Swedish Army?
____ with the Soviet Army?
____ with the North Vietnamese Army?
____ I could morally serve as a chaplain to no army besides that of the United States.

If a chaplain expected his role to be of significant military benefit to the army in which he served, then, I reasoned, he would be unwilling to serve in armies that might be enemies of the United States (and it should be noted that my questionnaires were all answered *before* the implementation of the Vietnam ceasefire). I received the following responses to item 48 (Table 5.2).[9]

Which Roles and Values the Chaplains Actually Affirm　　　　[93]

Table 5.2: Willingness of Chaplains to Serve as Chaplains with Various Armies

			Armies with which chaplains are willing to serve:		
	U.S. Army	U.S. Army and British Army	U.S. Army, British Army, and Swedish Army	U.S. Army, British Army, Swedish Army, and Soviet Army	U.S. Army, British Army, Swedish Army, Soviet Army, and North Vietnamese Army
Chaplains willing to serve	100%	91%	83%	63%	61%

Apparently chaplains are generally willing to perform their services in any army, undisturbed by thoughts that they might be aiding enemies of their homeland. For as a very high-ranking chaplain[10] said (having replied "yes" to all the armies listed in item 48), "Chaplains always serve *people,* never armies!"

ATTITUDES TOWARD CERTAIN ISSUES

I hope the reader is convinced that most chaplains are no more inclined than their civilian counterparts to perform a legitimating function for the military. This is the indication of my data; it is also the gist of most conversations I have had with army chaplains, active duty and retired. One should not get the idea, however, that the chaplains are in all things precisely like the civilian clergymen (and unlike their fellow army officers). There are, for example, several significant differences in the chaplains' attitudes toward certain issues. These attitudes were examined in items 33 through 37 in the questionnaire for military chaplains. In these items, as they are reproduced below, *the point marked A shows the mean rating for military commanders; B is for the civilian clergymen, and C is for the army chaplains:*

33. Overall, do you feel yourself more nearly oriented toward the values of nationalism or to those of a united world?

NATIONALISM　　　　　　　　　　　　　　　　　　　　　WORLD UNION

1　　　　　2　 A　　　 3　 C　　 B　 4　　　　　　　5

34. Do you tend to agree or disagree with the following statement? "In international relations, the interests of the United States should always come first."

AGREE　　　　　　　　　　　　　　　　　　　　　　　　DISAGREE

1　　　　　2　 A　　　 3　　 C　　 B　 4　　　　　　5

35. Do you agree or disagree with the following statement? "An insult to your honor should not be forgotten."

```
AGREE                                                    DISAGREE
                            A              C B
1           2           3   ↓          4   ↓ ↓           5
```

36. Do you think that you should remain very sensitive to human suffering, or do you feel you have to steel yourself to some extent so that you will be better able to carry out your duties in the face of such suffering?

```
REMAIN VERY                                          STEEL MYSELF
SENSITIVE                                            SOMEWHAT
                        B C                A
1           2           ↓ ↓   3            ↓   4           5
```

37. Do you feel it would be morally right to bomb (with nuclear weapons) the civilian population centers of an enemy nation in retaliation for similar attacks on our own population centers?

```
MORALLY RIGHT                                       MORALLY WRONG
TO BOMB                                             TO BOMB
                A                      C        B
1           2   ↓           3          ↓    4   ↓          5
```

The differences between clergymen and chaplains in questions 35 and 36 are only suggestive, but those in questions 33, 34, and 37 are rather substantial and are statistically significant well beyond the .05 level. Items 33 and 34 indicate that the chaplains are more nationalistically patriotic than the civilian clergymen. This was not an unexpected finding. Chaplains appear to be a rather patriotic group of men, and this was shown throughout their responses to my questionnaire. Item 37 indicates that chaplains may take a broader view than their civilian counterparts with respect to what actions are permissible in warfare. At any rate, our examination of issue-oriented attitudes has disclosed our first set of real differences between the chaplains and the civilian clergymen. An analysis of values and beliefs is even more revealing.

EVALUATION OF QUALITIES AND PERSONAL BELIEFS

In item 39 (questionnaire for military chaplains) I sought to determine chaplains' evaluations of the qualities for which I already had data from the clergymen and commanders.

39. It probably requires a very special sort of person to fulfill effectively the challenging vocation of the military chaplaincy. Below I have listed fourteen descriptive phrases. Some of them are appropriate for describing a military chaplain; others are inappropriate. Some may be neutral. In the spaces provided, please mark with a "1" the quality you feel is most important for a chaplain to possess. Mark the second-most important with a "2", and so on. Please mark all items.

Which Roles and Values the Chaplains Actually Affirm

___ boastful
___ strict
___ willing to forgive an offender again and again
___ willing to use violence to obtain justice
___ kind
___ feels killing in war is justified
___ believes in God as the final authority and absolute ruler over all men and nations
___ aggressive
___ meticulously avoids all "foul" or "improper" language
___ quick-tempered
___ unconditional in loyalty to the United States
___ loves enemies
___ gentle
___ dislikes involvement in any form of violence

Using the numbers with which you rated the above items, please tell which qualities you feel would be a positive help to the chaplain, which you feel would be neutral, and which you feel would be detrimental:

I believe that the qualities I marked with numbers *1* through___ would be helpful; those I marked with numbers___ through___ would be neutral; those I marked with numbers___ through *14* would be detrimental.

The four qualities over whose evaluation clergymen and commanders had agreed (kind, " 'foul' or 'improper' language," "quick-tempered," and "boastful") were also rated similarly by chaplains and consequently are ignored in our analysis. Ratings for the remaining 10 qualities are presented in Table 5.3, which gives mean ratings by chaplains; for comparison, see Tables 4.5 and 4.6, respectively, where we presented review ratings given by civilian clergymen and military commanders.

Once again we should note the similarity between the ratings of the clergymen and the chaplains. Let us remember, however, those four qualities we defined in the last chapter as critical:

A. Those rated positively by clergymen and negatively by commanders:
   1. "Willing to forgive an offender again and again."
   2. "Loves enemies."
B. Those rated negatively by clergymen and positively by commanders:
   1. "Feels killing in war is justified."
   2. "Unconditional in loyalty to the United States."

With respect to each of these qualities, the chaplains' ratings are significantly different[11] from those of the civilian clergymen; they have shifted in the direction of the military commanders. Furthermore, both the critical qualities rated negatively by the clergymen have moved up (though just barely) into the chaplains' neutral ratings. The next two chapters attempt to discover some reasons for these differences.

Table 5.3. Ratings of Qualities[a]

General Rating	Quality	by Military Chaplains Rating	Mean Score
"Positive"	God as final ruler	(1)	2.42
	Gentle	(2)	3.73
	Forgive again and again	(3)	4.97
	Loves enemies	(4)	5.86
"Neutral"	Aggressive	(5)	6.97
	Dislikes involvement in violence	(6)	8.21
	Strict	(7)	8.40
	Loyalty to United States	(8)	8.76
	Killing in war	(9)	9.53
"Negative"	Violence to obtain justice	(10)	10.20

a. Ratings have significance described in connection with Table 4.1.

CONFLICT WITH THE MILITARY?

The overall impression I have gained from my data is that despite the differences listed previously, army chaplains are, in their attitudes and actions, extremely similar to civilian clergymen—and different, in many ways, from their fellow officers. The question that now arises is whether the chaplains' views, different as they are from those of the commanders, ever bring them into conflict with the operation of the military. I addressed this question in item 26 on the questionnaire for military chaplains.

26. While a good chaplain's work is often helpful to the Army, there *may* be occasional instances in which a chaplain feels compelled by his religious convictions to do or say something that could prove detrimental to the efficient conduct of military operations. Have such instances actually arisen in the course of your ministry?

Of my respondents, 21.3% said that such incidents had arisen during their ministry, and 5.1% claimed to have knowledge of the type of conflict described, though they had not been personally involved. Another 13.4% said they had never heard of such cases but could nevertheless envision their occurrence. Fully 60.2% simply did not mention any occasion of chaplain-army conflict. Several of the chaplains who had personally faced the problem briefly related some of their experiences. *In no case did a chaplain think that the situation had arisen because of an intrinsic conflict of Christian teachings with military necessities.* Chaplains seemed rather to feel that the problem had occurred because of a commander's improper perception of military missions and necessities: If the commanders had not had a distorted view of their function, no conflict would have resulted. The following comments are illustrative:

> I felt it necessary to point out (remind?) *[sic]* our commander in Vietnam that our primary objective was to facilitate pacification, not kill "Gooks."—that military operations were a means toward an end. Fortunately, he agreed—and later made similar statements himself.[12]

and

> I objected to the burning and relocation of a village; though no one was hurt and the people were assisted, I still felt it was cruel and unnecessary.[13]

Item 26 was concerned with cases of conflict that had actually occurred. It became obvious from my responses that most chaplains did not know of any such instances (or were unwilling so to state). Since such responses were not unexpected, I decided to present the chaplains with two hypothetical situations describing potential clashes between the military and Christian ethical concepts. Item 44 was one such question.

44. In almost every war there have been reports of soldiers being ordered to kill enemy prisoners. Had a chaplain been present when such orders were given, what should he have done?

_____

_____

_____

The chaplains were adamant in their refusal to condone such orders. Only one man said he would take no action at all. Nearly three-quarters (71%) were prepared to make a very strong protest (i.e., tell the soldiers concerned that they must not follow the orders, then report the incident to the proper authorities); 7% favored the use of violence to stop the killing: "[The chaplain should] take a weapon and suggest they would have to go over him to get to the POW's,"[14] and "[The chaplain should have] stopped the shooting even if it meant killing the CO."[15]

As far as I could tell from their responses, none of the chaplains thought that a killing-of-prisoners situation constituted a conflict of military necessity with Christian ethical demands. Instead, and inarguably, they felt that orders to kill prisoners were outright illegal and were prohibited by military law as well as by the Christian ethic. Furthermore, several chaplains said that they simply could not imagine such orders being given in the United States Army. In contrast to this, however, no less than six chaplains claimed to have personal knowledge of such situations. One was personally familiar with the My Lai massacre. Another had brought formal charges against the perpetrators of a similar though much smaller incident. In each of the remaining four instances, *the chaplain concerned had successfully prevented the killing of the prisoners.* However one might interpret the duties and responsibilities of the chaplain, the actions of these four priests and ministers alone more than justify the existence of the Chaplain Corps.

My second hypothetical conflict situation was somewhat different.

45. Let us now consider an imaginary situation. An infantry battalion has been pulled out of the battle line for six weeks of rest and recuperation. At the end of this period, the battalion will again go back into combat. The battalion commander is sincerely worried about morale; the usual remedies of movies, ice cream, mail, and training have not worked, and the CO fears he will have to go back into the field with dispirited men. He therefore decides to set up (unofficially, of course) a temporary brothel for purposes of raising morale. The chaplain attached to the battalion gets wind of the idea. He talks with the battalion commander, attempting to explain that there will be no real, lasting gains in morale. Nevertheless, the CO is convinced that his idea will work. What should the chaplain do?

Here it is unfortunate that I cannot quote all of my respondents' comments, for many were quite interesting and displayed a real sense of humor. Most (88%) of the chaplains were prepared to make some form of protest, but there was little of the indignation brought out by the killing-of-prisoners situation. Again, many of the chaplains denied the possibility of such an occurrence: "No CO would take a chance like this—American newsmen would hang him before American MOTHERS!"[16] But other chaplains knew different: "I experienced same problem with a Transportation Battalion. (CO was a *pimp.*)"[17]

Some chaplains felt it was futile to fight such a venture:

> In my experience, the chaplains who have fought this situation have not won their battle and have paralyzed their effectiveness as chaplains.[18]

and

[The chaplain should do] nothing. The GI will get what he wants. The chaplain does not babysit.[19]

Some chaplains were ready to support the idea of a brothel (though often for reasons different from those of the CO): "Unfortunately I would agree with the CO only for different reasons—not morale, but health,"[20] and "Let's face it, girls are a great morale factor. I would encourage a medically inspected brothel."[21]

Perhaps the modal reply is best represented by the comments of a Catholic captain: "[I would] oppose the idea on higher up the chain [of command]. However, violations of sexual morality are not as serious as violations of justice. I would raise more hell about a lot of other things."[22] And then there was the chaplain who jokingly asked if my hypothetical brothel would offer a clerical discount.

SUMMARY

Chaplains and civilian clergymen, though they differ in some ways, are in general extremely similar. The interdenominational similarity we discovered among the civilian clergymen is found among the chaplains, even more emphatically. More important, the chaplains are no more anxious to "legitimate" the military than the civilian clergymen think they should be, despite the chaplains' seeming to be a bit more nationalistically patriotic. Chaplains evaluate certain qualities and personal beliefs very much like their civilian counterparts (though they are less willing than the clergymen to place a negative stamp on certain items valued very highly by military commanders). Most chaplains do not encounter situations in which God and Caesar come into direct conflict; furthermore, if they do, they tend to believe that "Caesar" has mistaken his own best interests and needs additional guidance from a friendly critic. If a chaplain thinks the army is doing something really wrong, he will protest, often quite strongly. And finally, even when these priests and ministers have to stand up against the military—and even when the military kicks back—my chaplain respondents really love the army: "I have been thrown off post by a famous general, been criticized by brigade chaplains and really cut down on a OER [officer-efficiency report] by a battalion CO because I followed my conscience but I still like the Army."[23]

NOTES

1. A Methodist colonel.
2. A Methodist major.
3. A Methodist captain.
4. A Lutheran major.
5. A Southern Baptist major; the capitals are his.
6. A Catholic captain.
7. A Methodist captain.
8. But note that on the other hand, with regard to the legitimating options the chaplains are even less military than the civilian clergymen! They want nothing to do with such tasks.
9. As would be expected, responses to this item were ordered almost perfectly as a Guttman scale. Thus those who checked "Swedish army" would also be willing to serve with the British and United States armies, and those who checked "North Vietnamese Army" would be willing to serve with all. There were only three misordered responses. One was from a Methodist respondent who was willing to serve as a chaplain to the North Vietnamese but not to the Soviet army. The other two were from Catholic chaplains who were willing to serve with the Swedish but not the British army.
10. A general officer whose denomination and precise grade shall remain unspecified.
11. In every case, $p < .01$.
12. A Southern Baptist lieutenant colonel. Many people who are unfamiliar with the military are ready to assume that it is an absolutely dictatorial organization in which discussion of plans and policy is never allowed. In many instances, however, commanders (especially the good ones) welcome discussion and even argument from their staff members. This quotation illustrates how one chaplain criticized his commander and—far from taking any action against the chaplain— the commander accepted and even appreciated the criticism. It is almost certain that this sort of problem resolution helps to keep chaplain-versus-army tension at the extremely low levels indicated by my respondents.
13. A Methodist captain.
14. A Lutheran colonel.
15. A Catholic captain.
16. A Catholic colonel.
17. A Catholic captain; the parenthetical emphasis is the chaplain's.
18. A Catholic major.
19. A Catholic captain.
20. A Methodist captain.
21. A Catholic captain.
22. A Catholic captain.
23. A Catholic captain.

Chapter 6

CURRENT VIEWS OF THE CHAPLAIN AND HIS ATTITUDES: A BRIEF SKETCH OF THE LITERATURE

Not only the personnel, but also the concept of the Christian Church have been taken over by the state for the purpose, in this specific instance, of winning wars.
    Waldo Burchard, on the military chaplaincy

The naval profession is much like the ministry. You dedicate your life to a purpose.... In the final analysis your aims and objects are quite as moral as any minister's.
    A retired naval captain, quoted by Morris Janowitz

HYPOTHESES EXPLICITLY DERIVED FROM THE WORKS OF SOCIAL PSYCHOLOGISTS

Thus far in our study we have been greatly concerned with the attitudes of chaplains toward a wide variety of tasks, qualities, and issues. We have discovered considerable variations in those attitudes, and we shall eventually attempt to explain the causes of such variation. First, however, we must know something about how attitudes are formed and changed.

Social psychologists have worked extensively to develop a theory of attitude change, and they have proposed many detailed hypotheses.[1] Unfortunately, however, the contesting hypothesis structures cannot make differentiated predictions outside the strictly controlled laboratory environment, and the field investigator is left with only the broadest outline of a theory. At its most fundamental level, the behavioral approach is based on central concepts of evolutionary theory. Any organism must be suited for survival in its environment, and if that environment changes in certain ways, the organism type must adapt itself accordingly or face extinction. Adaptation is not limited to the development (or suppression) of physical structures; behavioral adaptations can be equally important for survival. In the lower animals behavioral adaptations (like their structural counterparts) are generally evolved over numerous generations; however, in the higher vertebrates (including especially man) such adaptations are frequently made during the lifetime of an individual organism.[2] To survive in a new environment, an individual is compelled to change his behavior.

The effect of environment on *attitudes* is less direct. Environmental pressures demand only behavioral adaptations (we are not now concerned with biostructural evolution). However, the link between behavioral adaptation and attitude change is provided by dissonance theory, which postulates a human drive for cognitive consistency: If an individual performs an action X, conflicting with attitudes P, Q, and R (which the individual holds), dissonance will occur.[3] If the individual cannot undo or deny X, he can relieve the dissonance in one of two ways: He can convince himself that there is really no antithetical relationship between X and PQR, or he can change elements of the PQR attitude complex.[4] Furthermore, dissonance theorists recognize that attitudes are not absolutely independent of one another. An individual who "takes on" a new attitude is faced with the psychological task of ensuring that it will mesh with the complex of attitudes he already holds. Thus the drive for cognitive consistency not only presses for agreement of attitudes with behavior; it also demands a degree of logical congruence among attitudes.

Having briefly sketched a rather abstract theory of attitude change, we can employ that theory in explaining the attitude stances of our chaplains. Our first step is to formulate a few general hypotheses.

Hypothesis 1. If an organism developed in one environment is transferred to another, adaptations (behavioral and, through behavioral, attitudinal) will be greatest in areas where the differences between environment are greatest.

To become a chaplain, one must first be educated in a civilian seminary; one must be ordained as a clergyman of his parent denomination. He is then removed from the environment of the civilian parish (94% of my chaplain respondents served a civilian parish before beginning active duty) and transferred to the military environment. We may expect that in adapting to the latter environment he will change certain attitudes. Hypothesis 1 suggests that differences between the attitudes of chaplains and civilian clergymen will be greatest where differences between the attitudes of military commanders and civilian clergymen are greatest.

We are interested, of course, not only in the types of attitude that change but also in the backgrounds of men who change their attitudes. Here some of the field research done by social psychologists is of value. In *The Human Group,* George Homans suggests that "The more frequently persons interact with one another, the more alike in some respects their activities and their sentiments tend to become."[5] This could be true for several reasons. To begin, it takes some time for one person to learn the role demands of the other individuals with whom he interacts. If a person is to be accepted in a new role, he must learn to present himself in acceptable ways. He must be able to interpret the more or less subtle clues by which social environments present their demands for behavioral adaptations.[6] Thus early in his career, a chaplain may not completely recognize all the demands made by a military environment; he may think that the attitudes developed through his civilian clerical education are suited for an army career. Yet over time, the chaplain might be expected to learn, for instance, that the clergyman tasks he was taught in seminary are not those his fellow (nonchaplain) officers would wish him to stress. He may not change his priorities, but at least he will come to realize that commanders would prefer them changed.

Other research suggests an additional reason for the expectation that chaplains with extensive military experience will have more "military" attitudes. In his classic study of Bennington College, Theodore Newcomb discovered that although freshmen frequently arrived as political conservatives,[7] they generally shifted their attitudes over time to resemble the dominant campus liberal ideology.[8] Newcomb credited this change in part to long-term contact with the pervading college liberalism.[9] Newcomb also found, however, that the development of a "break" from the conservative home environment was equally important in the liberalizing of attitudes. The students who looked within the college for friendship and security changed their attitudes much more than those who looked beyond it (say, back to the conservative home environment).[10]

We could expect similar forces to be at work on our chaplains. While they are in the army, chaplains are in many ways removed from the kind of life led by civilian clergymen of their denominations. As they become increasingly distant from the environment of everyday-civilian-clergyman life, the pressures of that environment will also become increasingly remote, whereas the demands of the military environment will become more immediate and pressing. At this point, however, we must note that there remain throughout a chaplain's career numerous significant ties to the civilian center of his denomination. Therefore, though we shall expect a chaplain's attitudes to become more "military" as he gains more military experience, we must also qualify that expectation in light of the many sources of religious reinforcement the chaplain will maintain throughout his army career:

> *Hypothesis 2.* As a chaplain gains more military experience, his attitudes will increasingly resemble those of other military officers. *Qualification.* The tendency of this relationship will be weakened to the extent that the chaplain maintains contact with his civilian denomination and other extramilitary sources of religious and theological attitudes.

As the following chapter reveals, the testing of this hypothesis can become relatively complex.

Studies of complex organizations have shown that the more secure and important a person believes his position to be, the freer he may feel to deviate from sundry organizational norms:

> Occasionally we notice that the persons who stand highest in a group do not conform with undue strictness to some of the group norms, and controls are not seriously applied to them. Well-established members will suffer only a little joking when they break a rule, whereas newcomers will be severely punished with ridicule and scorn.... Up to a point, the surer a man is of his rank in a group, the less he has to worry about conforming to its norms.[11]

Conversely, on the very lowest rungs of the organizational ladder, there seems to be a similar degree of nonconformity. Those who perceive themselves as extremely important feel secure; those who perceive themselves as unimportant think they have nothing to lose. From these observations we can derive our third hypothesis.

> *Hypothesis 3.* Within an organization, conformity with the organizational norms will be greatest among those who credit themselves with medium importance; conformity will be less pronounced at the extremes of a subjective importance scale.

In testing this hypothesis we shall employ both direct and indirect measures of chaplains' subjective importance, derived from responses to the questionnaire for military chaplains.

HYPOTHESES DERIVED FROM WORKS DIRECTLY CONCERNED WITH CHAPLAINS

There is, of course, a wealth of information (and a small library of books) concerning social psychologists' research in the areas of attitude development and change. Thus it is most unfortunate that beyond the foregoing brief discussion, I am unable to apply it further to my attempt at explaining cases: The quasi-experimental research designs of the attitude-change psychologists require more closely controlled conditions than I, for reasons of space, resources, and especially population sensitivity, was able to produce in my questionnaire. Therefore, at this point we must pass beyond the theoretical works and examine some of the literature dealing explicitly with the military chaplaincy. Here I have found three major pieces that deserve our attention.[12]

1. Gordon Zahn, *The Military Chaplaincy: A Study of Role Tension in the Royal Air Force*. (Some of Professor Zahn's conclusions are reproduced as "Sociological Impressions of the Chaplaincy" in *Military Chaplains: From a Religious Military To a Military Religion*, edited by Harvey G. Cox.)
2. Waldo W. Burchard, *The Role of the Military Chaplain*. (This hard-to-find, unpublished dissertation is well summarized as "Role Conflicts of Military Chaplains" in *American Sociological Review*.
3. Chaplain (Col.) Clifford E. Keys, Jr., USA, *Student Research Project 86: An Evaluation of Certain Factors Affecting the Retention Rate of Career Chaplains in the United States Army*.

The book by Zahn has been mentioned in a previous chapter. *The Military Chaplaincy* began with two hypotheses: (1) role tension (clergyman vs. military officer) exists; (2) such tension is generally resolved in favor of the military role dimension.[13] As we discovered, however, the first hypothesis is substantiated only by Zahn's theological "proof" that tension must exist between Christianity and certain demands a state might make in wartime.[14] This midstream change of methodologies (as I explain in reference to the work by Burchard) renders much of what is said in Zahn's otherwise excellent book less than vital to any serious social science research project.

It is more difficult to evaluate concisely the dissertation by Waldo Burchard. It was a most ambitious project. At the onset, the author wished to examine the attitudes of chaplains, enlisted men, officers, and veterans, from all branches of the American armed forces, on war, peace, and Christianity. He soon found that sending questionnaires to the officers was "impossible" (perhaps in the early 1950s this was indeed the case), and his sampling of the other populations was in many ways inadequate. The veterans (N = 270) were contacted through San Francisco area veterans' organizations. Since Burchard was not allowed to distribute his survey instrument on government property, he passed out 270 questionnaires to 270 enlisted men he happened to find in San Francisco USOs and YMCAs. The author freely admits the biased nature of these samples and spends only some 40 pages (of his 400-page opus) in discussing them. None of his findings in these areas are of any particular interest to our present discussion.

Burchard's chaplain interviews form the heart of his dissertation. These interviews were conducted with 36 active-duty chaplains and 35 former chaplains, again in the San Francisco Bay area. The dissertation began by viewing the chaplain as a man with two sets of roles: those of a clergyman and those of a military officer. Since Burchard further held that conflict between these two role sets existed, he was concerned chiefly with the manner in which this conflict could be resolved. He listed three possible solutions. First, the chaplain could virtually abandon one role set or the other. Second, he could rationalize the content of one or both role sets, to prevent them from conflicting. Third, he could avoid conflict by "... withdrawing to 'compartments' so that at any given time one role is active and the others are passive."[15] Burchard seems to feel that this third process is the most frequent method of conflict resolution:

> It appears that the chaplain regards himself as operating in a moral context while he is conducting religious services or performing other tasks which are associated in his mind with the work of a clergyman, and which are not covered by military regulations, but not while dealing with commanding officers, fellow officers, channels of communication, and in other non-religious situations which are covered by the regulations. In religious situations he is guided by religious values; in other situations by other values.[16]

In short, Burchard accuses chaplains of what Dietrich Bonhoeffer called "two-spheres thinking"; furthermore, he seems to feel that chaplains allow the military to define by its sole authority both the contents and the limits of its proper sphere![17]

I do not fully understand the connection between Burchard's affirmation of the "compartmentalization" hypothesis and his hard data—

nor, I feel, does he. It seems more probable that he simply assumed it as the only possible explanation of two "facts": (1) there is conflict between the roles of clergyman and military officer, and (2) chaplains do not feel the conflict.[18] (Therefore, they must have resolved it; therefore, since it seems the most likely way out, they must have compartmentalized.)

In ascertaining the first of his two "facts," however, Burchard is making the same methodological error as Zahn. Indeed, he is making the mistake in an obvious perhaps even tasteless manner that will help to illustrate the problem most clearly. Early in his dissertation Burchard presents the "fact" of Christian-versus-soldier tension and also offers the compartmentalization hypothesis as a way out. Here he is speaking of the Christian who is also a soldier:

> His position as a Christian requires him to be generous, reverent, forgiving and kind, to love his enemies and to do good to those who would harm him; his position as a member of the armed forces requires him to be aggressive, vengeful, cruel, cunning and hateful. How can one have all these qualities at once? The answer is that he cannot.... How, then will he act? He will play his role in any given instance as though it were his only role, excluding contradictory and competing elements for the time.[19]

There certainly does appear to be a conflict between the "generous, reverent, forgiving... kind" Christian and the "aggressive, vengeful, cruel, cunning... hateful" soldier; therefore, the "fact" of clergyman-versus-military officer conflict is proved, right? Wrong! Burchard simply combines inept theology with a slanderous misinterpretation of the military ethic to prepare his readers to accept the above-quoted passage as proof.[20]

First of all, it is simply not true that pacifism is the only theologically defensible Christian view of war. The Old Testament glorifies war to an embarrassing degree, and the New Testament nowhere explicitly condemns it. Virtually none of the great theologians have been absolute pacifists (though some, Karl Barth, for example, have come extremely close); there was insufficient biblical warrant, and besides, if a theologian denied that God could command participation in war, he would be denying the *potentia Dei absoluta*! Similarly, it is very difficult to build a watertight theological argument that there must even be tension between Christianity and "the World."[21] Furthermore, even if it could be proved theologically that tension must exist between Christianity and the state (or even if it could be proved that pacifism were the only acceptable doctrine relating to war), one could not justly say that a chaplain who supports the state unconditionally has sold out his clerical values. One might say he was a heretic or perhaps a sinner, but no one could prove that he had been actively "co-opted to promote the aims of the state."[22] There can be no doubt of the existence of large numbers of ordained Christian clergymen who believe on *theological grounds* (correctly or incorrectly) that it is just for a Christian to serve his country in military combat.[23] Could not one logically argue that chaplains were simply clergymen of that religious persuasion?

We are now ready to take a quick look at the final work on our list. The thesis by Chaplain Keys is chiefly concerned with a question only indirectly connected to the present research. Overall, the army retains only about 18% of the junior officers completing their first term of service; however 52% of the chaplains completing their initial service elect to remain on active duty. What accounts for this extremely high retention rate?

Most of the factors investigated are of no significance to us here, but one is very interesting and may be crucial to this study. Chaplain Keys insists that *far from being in conflict with the military life style, many religious values are actually emphasized in the army.*[24] The chaplain does not see the soldier's life as characterized by blood lust, cruelty, and idolatrous state worship. Instead, he emphasizes soldierly qualities of unselfishness, courage, and disciplined dedication to a cause that transcends the self. On the other hand, the chaplain accepts a theology that (1) is not strictly pacifistic and (2) does *not* emphasize the form of church-state relationship Niebuhr classified as "Christ against culture."[25] This line of thought may seem to lead to the position of a "rationalization" hypothesis: that chaplains reinterpret both Christian and military values until the two sets are seen as congruent. I shall insist, however, that such need not be the case. I have already shown (Chapter 2) that American Christianity has been prone to develop a sort of *theologica gloria* emphasizing that service to America (including military service) is service to God. Furthermore, the average American soldier has seldom been widely regarded as "vengeful, cruel, cunning, and hateful."[26] In short, it appears to me that the American military-religious environment might produce clergymen who, when recruited into the chaplaincy, would not need to rationalize, compartmentalize, or otherwise change their attitudes at all. Thus we can posit a final hypothesis.

Hypothesis 4. Many chaplains will tend to see military values as similar or identical to the values they had developed as Christians and clergymen before becoming chaplains. For these chaplains the military will not constitute a new and different moral environment requiring behavioral (thereby attitudinal) adaptation; therefore, their attitudes will not be changed.

It will not be possible to test this supposition directly, though it bears heavily on the problem of explaining the variation in degrees of "civilianness" or "militariness" among chaplains. If Hypothesis 4 is indeed true, the explanation offered in Hypotheses 2 and 3 will account for very little variation, not necessarily because the hypotheses are unsound in themselves but rather because the premise on which they are based—a change of environment—does not obtain.

NOTES

1. See, for example, Charles A. Kiesler et al., *Attitude Change*, pp. 90, ff.
2. Learning theorists, who are concerned with this type of behavior change, like to speak in terms of "rewards" and "punishments" provided by the changing organism's objective environment (ibid., p. 90).
3. Aside from the foregoing definition, it is difficult to say in any concrete terms what dissonance is or how it brings about attitudinal change. Perhaps it would be not inaccurate to describe dissonance as a sort of psychological "discomfort" resulting from cognitive inconsistency.
4. See Elliot Aronson, "Dissonance Theory: Progress and Problems," in *Theories of Cognitive Consistency,* by Robert P. Abelson et al. Of course it is not absolutely necessary that the dissonance be relieved at all. Some individuals, in fact, apparently can stand rather high dissonance levels. Nevertheless, a student of evolution theory might consider the tendency for an actor's attitudes to shape themselves so that his actions will be subjectively approved. For an animal that has developed "consciousness," there is a great deal of survival utility in *liking* to do what must be done.
5. George Homans, *The Human Group*, p. 120.
6. See Erving Goffman, *The Presentation of Self.*
7. Theodore M. Newcomb, *Personality and Social Change*, pp. 9-10.
8. Ibid., p. 24.
9. Ibid., pp. 24, 54.
10. Ibid., p. 107; see also pp. 64 and 156.
11. Homans, pp. 143-144; see also John W. Thibaut and Harold H. Kelley, *The Social Psychology of Groups*, p. 250.
12. A fourth major work deserves at least passing comment. It is *A Comparative Study of the Opinions of Navy Chaplains and Their Commanding Officers on*

Role Expectations, Deficiencies, and Preferred In-Service Education for Navy Chaplains by Chaplain Alexander B. Aronis, U.S.N. The thesis was mainly concerned with chaplain deficiencies and their rectification through proper education, and little of its discussion was directly relevant to our present concern. Nevertheless, Chaplain Aronis examined six chaplain tasks, one of which might be considered a "legitimating" option. I am happy to say that his chaplains, like mine, placed the "legitimating" option at the bottom of their list—though the commanders indicated that they might have preferred a higher rating (see Aronis, especially pp. 74 and 88).

13. Gordon Zahn, *The Military Chaplaincy*, pp. 31-32.
14. Ibid., p. 18.
15. Waldo Burchard, *The Role of the Military Chaplain*, p. 6.
16. Burchard, "Role Conflicts of Military Chaplains," p. 531.
17. See especially Dietrich Bonhoeffer, *Letters and Papers from Prison*, pp. 142, 191. In this respect, however, Dr. Burchard should be most cautious, for early in the dissertation he produces his own affirmation of Bonhoeffer's pet-peeve heresy: "There is no escape from dualism in the Judeo-Christian tradition. On the one side is the world of the flesh; on the other side is the world of the spirit" (Burchard, *The Role of the Military Chaplain*, p. 16).
18. Burchard, *The Role of the Military Chaplain*, p. 296.
19. Ibid., p. 13.
20. Besides the academic necessity, I have three reasons for being unwilling to slide over this lightly. (1) Burchard slanders the army and the chaplains, and I have become tied by affection to both. (2) He virtually forces me to explain that pacifism (to which I very strongly tend) is not the only theologically defensible way of looking at warfare. (3) I think he may have hurt my return rates. Had I been a chaplain familiar with Burchard's work, I would not have returned another social scientist's questionnaire, to protect my views from distortion.
21. See H. Richard Niebuhr, *Christ and Culture*.
22. Burchard, *The Role of the Military Chaplain*, p. 17.
23. See Niebuhr, *Christ and Culture*, especially pp. 83-115.
24. Clifford E. Keys, Jr., *Student Research Project 86*, p. 5. Similarly, in *The Soldier and the State*, Samuel Huntington shows that a strong case can be made for the congruence of military and religious values. In *The Professional Soldier*, Morris Janowitz suggests that the similar values emphasized by military and religious professions attract the same sort of person to both careers (see especially pp. 114-115).
25. Niebuhr; especially pp. 45-82.
26. Burchard, *The Role of the Military Chaplain*, p. 13. Furthermore, when the American soldier has displayed the above-mentioned characteristics, his conduct has been regarded (at least by my chaplain respondents, see Chapter 5) as a perversion of the military (as well as the religious) ethic.

Chapter 7

CHAPLAINS, TOO, ARE PEOPLE, OR

THE NONEXPLANATION OF VARIANCE

I think that the position of chaplain in the military is a cultural development.

A survey respondent

Let us now examine the four hypotheses introduced in Chapter 6, defining certain terms and deriving indices and variables as required.

THE FIRST HYPOTHESIS

Hypothesis 1. If an organism developed in one environment is transferred to another, adaptation (behavioral and, through behavioral, attitudinal) change will be greatest in areas where the differences between environments are greatest.

We have already suggested that the chaplain may be thought of as a civilian clergyman transferred to a military environment. Furthermore, we have defined differences between the two environments in terms of differences between mean response scores of clergymen and commanders. Therefore, if Hypothesis 1 is correct, we should expect *differences between clergyman and chaplain attitudes* to be positively correlated with *differences between clergyman and commander attitudes*. This hypothesis was tested with respect to each of the three sets of attitude-related items on my questionnaires.

The Task Options

25. Today's military chaplain has many important tasks to fulfill. Below I have listed eleven functions which various chaplains have seen as very important. Please mark the item *you* feel is most important with a "1", the second-most important item with a "2", and so on. Please mark all items. If you feel that any item describes a function *not* appropriate for a

chaplain, please mark it with an "X". Please order the functions as you would in a combat situation.

____ The chaplain helps men gain the spiritual strength that will enable them to perform their duties more effectively despite the suffering and hardships of military operations.

____ The chaplain is concerned with evangelism and conversation.

____ The chaplain helps to bolster the troops' fighting spirit and morale.

____ The chaplain counsels troops on personal problems.

____ The chaplain preaches a message of reconciliation, emphasizing that even the enemy must not be hated.

____ The chaplain helps troops make the difficult personal adjustments required by extended operations in a hostile environment.

____ The chaplain prays that God will grant victory.

____ The chaplain administers the sacraments and conducts worship services.

____ The chaplain visits with and ministers to the sick and wounded.

____ The chaplain acts as a special staff officer advising the commanding officer.

____ The chaplain stresses that obedience to the properly constituted authorities is a Christian duty.

For each of the 11 items in this question, two scores were calculated.[1]

1. Environmental difference scores were differences between the mean ratings of the civilian clergymen and the commanding officers.
2. Attitudinal adaptation scores were differences between the mean ratings of the civilian clergymen and the chaplains.

As Hypothesis 1 leads us to expect, environmental difference scores were quite highly correlated with attitudinal adaptation scores with $R = .73$. The correlation coefficient was significant well beyond the .05 level.

The Opinion Options

33. Overall, do you feel yourself more nearly oriented toward the values of nationalism or to those of a united world?

NATIONALISM				WORLD UNION
1	2	3	4	5

34. Do you tend to agree or disagree with the following statement? "In international relations, the interests of the United States should always come first."

AGREE				DISAGREE
1	2	3	4	5

35. Do you agree or disagree with the following statement? "An insult to your honor should not be forgotten."

AGREE   DISAGREE

1   2   3   4   5
....

36. Do you think that you should remain very sensitive to human suffering, or do you feel you have to steel yourself to some extent so that you will be better able to carry out your duties in the face of such suffering?

REMAIN VERY   STEEL MYSELF
SENSITIVE   SOMEWHAT

1   2   3   4   5
....

37. Do you feel it would be morally right to bomb (with nuclear weapons) the civilian population centers of an enemy nation in retaliation for similar attacks on our own population centers?

MORALLY RIGHT   MORALLY WRONG
TO BOMB   TO BOMB

1   2   3   4   5
....

As with the task-option question, environmental difference scores (mean scores for civilian clergymen minus mean scores for military officers) and attitudinal adaptation scores (mean scores for civilian clergymen minus mean scores for chaplains) were calculated for each item. Once again the scores were positively correlated ($R = .43$), though partly because of the small N, the coefficient was not statistically significant.

The Quality Options

39. It probably requires a very special sort of person to fulfill effectively the challenging vocation of the military chaplaincy. Below I have listed fourteen descriptive phrases. Some of them are appropriate for describing a military chaplain; others are inappropriate. Some may be neutral. In the spaces provided, please mark with a "1" the quality you feel is most important for a chaplain to possess. Mark the second-most important with a "2", and so on. Please mark all items.

___ boastful
___ strict
___ willing to forgive an offender again and again
___ willing to use violence to obtain justice
___ kind
___ feels killing in war is justified
___ believes in God as the final authority and absolute ruler over all men and nations
___ aggressive
___ meticulously avoids all "foul" or "improper" language
___ quick-tempered
___ unconditional in loyalty to the United States
___ loves enemies
___ gentle
___ dislikes involvement in any form of violence

Once more the environmental difference scores and attitudinal adaptation scores were calculated, and once again they were positively correlated—in this case, quite strongly ($R = .87$; the coefficient is significant well beyond the .05 level).

Summary Discussion of Hypothesis 1

It seems at this point that our first hypothesis is borne out by the data. Differences between clergyman and chaplain attitudes are at greatest variance over the issues concerning which clergyman and commander attitudes are also most different. Thus it appears that differences between clergymen and chaplains are not simply random but instead are related to the demands of the military environment. Our next two hypotheses address this relationship.

THE SECOND HYPOTHESIS

Hypothesis 2. As a chaplain gains more military experience, his attitudes will increasingly resemble those of other military officers. *Qualification.* The tendency of this relationship will be weakened to the extent that the chaplain maintains contact with his civilian denomination and other sources of religious and theological attitudes.

Developing an Index of "Militariness" (The Dependent Variable)

To investigate the hypothesis that chaplains become more military in their attitudes, we must first develop an index of attitudinal "militariness" that can serve as our dependent variable. In this task I began with the familiar three sets of attitudinal questionnaire items and developed a series of four variables that I felt were related to the concept of "militariness."

Mean legitimacy score. This variable was constructed from the three legitimation-of-suffering options over which the ratings of clergymen and commanders diverged rather widely:

> (a) The chaplain helps men gain the spiritual strength that will enable them to perform their duties more effectively despite the suffering and hardships of military operations.
> (b) The chaplain helps to bolster the troops' fighting spirit and morale.
> (c) The chaplain helps troops make the difficult personal adjustments required by extended operations in a hostile environment.

For each chaplain the ratings given these three options were added, and the sum was divided by 3; this constituted a chaplain's *mean legitimacy score.* Since military officers rated these options as more important (i.e., they gave them lower numbers) than did the civilian clergymen, a *smaller* mean legitimacy score indicates a higher degree of "militariness."

Mean prophetic score. This variable was constructed from the two "prophetic" task options:

(a) The chaplain is concerned with evangelism and conversion.
(b) The chaplain preaches a message of reconciliation, emphasizing that even the enemy must not be hated.

For each chaplain the ratings given these two options were added, and the sum was divided by 2; this constituted a chaplain's *mean prophetic score.* Larger mean prophetic scores indicate higher degrees of "militariness."

Mean five-item opinion rating. As the name indicates, this variable was constructed from the five scaled-response items on my questionnaires.

33. Overall, do you feel yourself more nearly oriented toward the values of nationalism or to those of a united world?

NATIONALISM   WORLD UNION

1   2   3   4   5
....

For item 33, each chaplain was given a score A such that if he circled "1," $A = 5$; if he circled "2," $A = 4, \ldots$, and if he circled "5," $A = 1$.

34. Do you tend to agree or disagree with the following statement? "In international relations, the interests of the United States should always come first."

AGREE   DISAGREE

1   2   3   4   5
....

For item 34 each chaplain was given a score B, derived in the same manner as A.

35. Do you agree or disagree with the following statement? "An insult to your honor should not be forgotten."

AGREE   DISAGREE

1   2   3   4   5
....

For option 35 each chaplain was given a score *C*, derived in the same manner as *A* and *B*.

36. Do you think that you should remain very sensitive to human suffering, or do you feel you have to steel yourself to some extent so that you will be better able to carry out your duties in the face of such suffering?

REMAIN VERY SENSITIVE				STEEL MYSELF SOMEWHAT
1	2	3	4	5

For item 36 each chaplain was given a score *D*, equal to the number he had circled.

37. Do you feel it would be morally right to bomb (with nuclear weapons) the civilian population centers of an enemy nation in retaliation for similar attacks on our own population centers?

MORALLY RIGHT TO BOMB				MORALLY WRONG TO BOMB
1	2	3	4	5

For item 37 each chaplain was given a score *E*, derived in the same manner as *A*, *B*, and *C* (but *not D*).

The mean five-item option rating was defined for each chaplain as

$$\frac{(A + B + C + D + E)}{5}$$

Note that higher mean five-item opinion ratings indicate a higher degree of "militariness."

Quality and belief score. In Chapter 4 we identified as critical four qualities from item 25 (questionnaire for military officers). Two were rated positive by the clergymen and negative by the commanders:

(a) willing to forgive an offender again and again. (This option was given a value *W*, equal to the number with which a chaplain marked it.)
(b) loves enemies. (This option was given a value *X*, equal to the number with which a chaplain marked it.)

The other two were rated *negative* by the clergymen and *positive* by the commanders:

(a) feels killing in war is justified. (This option was given a value *Y*, equal to the number with which a chaplain marked it.)

(b) unconditional in loyalty to the United States. (This option was given a value Z, equal to the number with which a chaplain marked it.)

Each chaplain was given a *quality and belief score* calculated as follows: $W + X - Y - Z$. The commanders, of course, had given the first two options low importance ratings (i.e., for them W and X would have been large numbers) and the last two high importance ratings (i.e., their values of Y and Z would have been small). The civilian clergymen had done just the opposite. Thus a high quality and belief score indicates that a chaplain has a high degree of "militariness."

The overall militariness index. Numerous calculations were made using the four indices just described as dependent variables for a variety of quantitative techniques. My results indicated that each of these variables was in some sense measuring the same thing—which we have called "militariness." Therefore it is reasonable to combine the four variables into one overall index, thereby canceling out some of the (hopefully) random measurement-error present in each of the separate, more limited variables. An *overall militariness index* was calculated as follows. For each chaplain, values of his mean prophetic score, his mean five-item option rating, and his quality and belief score were summed, and from that total, the value for his mean legitimacy score was subtracted.[2] Clearly, *higher values for the overall militariness index indicate greater degrees of "militariness."* This index has a maximum possible range that stretches from -33.5 to 39. Its actual range for my chaplains is -33.3 to 30.6; its actual mean is -5.67, and its standard deviation is 10.0. The attempt to predict degrees of "militariness" in particular chaplains (using the independent variables described below) works best when the overall militariness index is used as the dependent variable, and our discussion of prediction attempts is confined to models in which that general index is so used.

Defining Independent Variables

Military experience independent variables. Four variables were used as indicators of military experience. There were (a) the number of years an individual had been a chaplain (henceforth called years service), (b) the individual's rank (rank), (c) the number of months an individual had served in a combat zone (combat), and (d) the number of service schools an individual had attended (service schools).[3]

Independent variables concerned with nonmilitary sources of religious and theological attitudes. Hypothesis 2 suggests that the tendency for increased military experience to lead to increased "militariness" is weakened to the extent that the chaplain maintains contact with his civilian denomination and other sources of religious and theological attitudes. Six different items on the questionnaire for military chaplains were used in an attempt to measure the extent of extramilitary religious reinforcement:

(a) the number of religious periodicals to which the chaplain subscribed (periodicals),
(b) the number of hours per week spent studying religious and theological materials (study),
(c) the number of hours per week spent in private prayer and devotion (prayer),
(d) the number of times per year the chaplain preaches to a civilian congregation (civilian preaching),
(e) the frequency with which the chaplain receives communications from the civilian officials of his denomination (communication),[4]
(f) the proposition of a chaplain's clergyman friends who are also chaplains (friends).[5]

The Testing of Hypothesis 2

The model. For Hypothesis 2 I posited a regression model specifying that *militariness depends on years service, rank, combat experience, attendance at service schools, and the six measures of religious value reinforcement, listed previously.*[6] Since our hypothesis predicts an increase in "militariness" with increased military experience, the regression coefficients for the military-experience variables should be positive. Conversely, since the hypothesis predicts decreased "militariness" in chaplains who maintain extramilitary sources of religious reinforcement, we would expect the remaining six regression coefficients to be negative.

Findings. The following variables were found to be without statistical significance,[7] taken singly or in any combination: combat, periodicals, communication, service schools, prayer, friends, and civilian preaching.

The regression coefficient for rank was significant, but its sign was negative, indicating that other things being equal, higher ranking chaplains are likely to be *less* military than their lower ranking colleagues. Discussion of why this may be the case is relegated to a later section.

The regression coefficients for variable years service and study are significant, and their signs are as predicted by Hypothesis 2. For each additional year of service a chaplain's overall militariness score increases by about 0.27 point (assuming that study is held constant). For each additional hour of weekly study, a chaplain's overall militariness score decreases by about 0.13 point (assuming that years service is held constant). Since the overall militariness score has a range of over 60 points (and its standard deviation is 10.0), we can see that the effects of years service and study are quite small. *Taken together, they account for less than 3% of the total variance in overall militariness.* If Hypothesis 2 is indeed valid, it is given only scant support by the data from my questionnaire returns.

THE THIRD HYPOTHESIS

Hypothesis 3. Within an organization, conformity with the organizational norms will be greatest among those who credit themselves with medium degrees of importance; conformity will be less pronounced at the extremes of a subjective importance scale.

The Dependent Variable, General "Militariness"

Again, our overall militariness score constitutes the dependent variable.

The Independent Variables, Subjective Importance

We selected the following independent variables: rank, medals, campaigns, importance, expected enlisted rating, and expected commander rating.

We have seen that higher rank was significantly associated with lower militariness. Perhaps, then, we should consider rank not as a variable of military experience but rather as a variable of subjective importance. Higher ranking chaplains, according to Hypothesis 3, may feel more secure about their military position; thus they may feel freer to diverge from military attitude definitions, and therefore their overall militariness scores may be lower. Recall the observation of George Homans, "Up to a point, the surer a man is of his rank in a group, the less he has to worry about conforming to its norms."[8]

Medals, the second independent variable for Hypothesis 3 was similar to the first. It was felt that chaplains who had received a large number of awards and decorations would have gained enough "eccentricity credits" to allow greater deviation from the military attitude structure. Therefore chaplains with more medals were expected to have lower overall militariness scores.

The third independent variable (campaigns) was developed after a careful examination of militariness scores for chaplains who had had various amounts of combat experience. It was found that chaplains (1) with little or no combat experience and (2) with a very great deal of combat experience were noticeably less "military" than chaplains who had spent only a moderate amount of time in a combat zone. It seemed reasonable to expect that chaplains who had had little combat experience would see themselves as peripheral to the military environment, thus would feel free to criticize it. Chaplains with a moderate amount of experience would be less likely to criticize, whereas chaplains with a great deal of time under fire would not feel overly constrained by petty demands for conformity, thus would be likely to express nonmilitary attitudes.

Since these expectations were right in line with Hypothesis 3, a variable (campaigns) was constructed to express the expected nonlinear effect of time in combat. Chaplains who had spent less than a full tour in a combat zone (less than 12 months) were given a code of "0." Chaplains with one tour (12-13 months) received a code value of "1." Chaplains with more than one but less than two tours (14-20 months) were given a code value of "2." Chaplains with two (but no more) tours (21-25 months) were given a code value of "1," and chaplains with more than two tours (26-70 months, in the case of my population) were given a code value of "0." According to Hypothesis 3, we expect higher code values of campaigns to be associated with higher overall militariness scores.

The fourth independent variable (importance) for Hypothesis 3 was derived from item 29 on the questionnaire for military chaplains. If the respondent marked the option "Chaplain" with a "1," he was given a value of "0" for the variable importance. Other responses were coded as follows:

29. In what order of overall importance would *you* rate the following personnel, who might be in or attached to an infantry battalion? (Mark the most important with a "1", the second-most important with a "2", and so on. Please mark all items. To be more specific, let me suggest that the battalion is in a garrison situation but may be called into combat at very short notice; let me suggest, in fact, that the battalion under consideration is one from the 82 Airborne Division.)

____ S-1
____ Chaplain
____ Assistant S-3

____ Medical Officer
____ Maintenance Officer
____ Sergeant-Major

Chaplains, Too, Are People, or The Nonexplanation of Variance [121]

Option "Chaplain" Marked	Value Coded for Importance
2	1
3	2
4	2
5	1
6	0

According to Hypothesis 3, we expect higher values of importance to be associated with higher overall militariness scores.

The fifth independent variable (expected enlisted rating) was derived from item 30 of the questionnaire for military chaplains in a manner analogous to the derivation of importance.

30. In what order of importance would the *typical enlisted man* (of the same battalion) rate the following?

___ S-1 ___ Medical Officer
___ Chaplain ___ Maintenance Officer
___ Assistant S-3 ___ Sergeant-Major

Option "Chaplain" Marked	Value Coded for Expected Enlisted Rating
1	0
2	1
3	2
4	2
5	1
6	0

According to Hypothesis 3, we expect higher values of expected enlisted rating to be associated with higher overall militariness scores.

The sixth independent variable (expected commander rating) was derived from item 31 of the questionnaire for military chaplains in a manner analogous to the derivation of importance and expected enlisted rating.

31. In what order of importance would the *typical battalion commander* (of the same unit) rate the following?

___ S-1 ___ Medical Officer
___ Chaplain ___ Maintenance Officer
___ Assistant S-3 ___ Sergeant-Major

Option "Chaplain Marked	Value Coded for Expected Commander Rating
1	0
2	1
3	2
4	2
5	1
6	0

According to Hypothesis 3, we expect higher values of expected commander rating to be associated with high overall militariness scores.

The Testing of Hypothesis 3

The model. The regression model posited for Hypothesis 3 specified that *militariness depends on rank, medals, campaigns, importance, expected enlisted rating, and expected commander rating.*[9] According to Hypothesis 3, militariness should decrease with increases in rank and medals; therefore, we should expect the regression coefficients associated with those two variables to be negative. According to Hypothesis 3, we should expect the other regression coefficients to be positive.

Findings. The only statistically significant regression coefficient was the one associated with the variable campaigns.[10] The value of this coefficient is 3.2. The least square line defined by this coefficient (and an intercept term, -8.33) may be said to account for about 2.5% of the variance in overall militariness found among my chaplain respondents.

A COMBINED MODEL

Before we proceed to a discussion of the fourth hypothesis developed in this chapter, we should be aware of the total amount of militariness variance explained by the combined effects of the independent variables used to examine Hypotheses 2 and 3.

The Dependent Variable

Once again the dependent variable is the overall militariness score.

The Independent Variables

The independent variables are those which have been found to have significant effects on overall militariness scores (years service, study, and campaigns) plus those two additional variables whose effects bordered on statistical significance (rank and importance).

Testing the Combined Effects of Hypotheses 2 and 3

The model. To test the combined effects of Hypotheses 2 and 3, I posited a regression model in which militariness depends on years service, study, campaigns, rank, and importance.[11] As explained in the discussion of previous models, we would expect the regression coefficients associated with years service, campaigns, and importance to be positive. Conversely, we would expect the coefficients associated with study and rank to be negative.

Findings. In this case all the variables except study contribute significantly to explaining the variance in overall militariness.[12] *However, their combined effects (which represent, insofar as we can measure them, the combined effects of Hypotheses 2 and 3) explain only about 7.7% of the total variance in militariness.*

THE FOURTH HYPOTHESIS

Hypothesis 4. Many chaplains will tend to see military values as similar or identical to the values they had developed as Christians and clergymen before becoming chaplains. For these chaplains the military will not constitute a new and different moral environment requiring behavioral (thereby attitudinal) adaptations.

The necessary explanations of Hypotheses 2 and 3 are long, and the variable definitions are complex and difficult to hold in mind. The models therefore seem somewhat abstract, and the specific results are difficult to interpret. Yet there are two important conclusions to be drawn from the foregoing discussion.

1. I have made a reasonably thorough attempt to use military background factors to explain the variation of "militariness" among chaplains.
2. That attempt has quite convincingly failed.

As is so frequently the case in social science research, the result of intensive (even painful) statistical analysis is not an answer but rather a more interesting statement of the original question: after we have incorporated 15 military background variables,[13] more than 90% of the variation in "militariness" among chaplains remains unexplained. What is going on? It is, of course, quite easy to conceive of additional variables that might aid in the explanation of our 90% residual variance. What kind of seminary education did the chaplain receive? (Did he read Rauschenbusch or Barth?) What was the religious and psychological atmosphere of the home in which he was reared? (Did they pray before meals?) What was the chaplain's background by "SES"? (poor? rich? black? southern? white collar?) Potentially, the number of variables is almost limitless, but for my purposes it would not be worthwhile to draw up another long list. This study could swiftly lose its central thrust and become a sociological tract, a pseudo-experiment in social psychology, or (worst of all) a statistical fishing expedition. Basically, then, I am not attempting to identify the background or attitudinal variables that might explain our 92.3% residual "militariness" variance. *I am interested instead in why military background variables explained only a very small portion of the variation in the attitudinal characteristics we called "militariness."*

Thus I have restated the original question examined by Hypotheses 2 and 3. Now I am prepared to offer an answer, though I shall move back a step or two from the secure realm of F-tests and correlation coefficients. The explanation is based (1) on more subtle clues within the data (hence clues subject to more serious misinterpretation); and (2) on readings and conversations that go beyond my questionnaire returns (and may therefore be in some sense alien to the real feelings of my respondents). Forewarned, the reader should be prepared to disagree, and to test his disagreement in an appropriately controlled research project. Nevertheless, at least until the hard data say otherwise, I place a good deal of my trust in the explanation that follows.

In simplest terms, I hold that Hypothesis 4 is correct; for the clergyman who becomes a chaplain, the military simply does not constitute a new and different religious environment requiring behavioral (thereby attitudinal) adaptations. This is true for both theological and sociological reasons.

In the first place, the chaplain should feel that his attitudes, insofar as they are Christian attitudes, transcend the differences in environmental "demands." Let us assume, for illustration, that at least in certain situations, a chaplain holds respect for human life as the Christian norm for all people. Let us also assume that most regular military officers hold that respect for human life should never be allowed to conflict with the necessity of accomplishing a given military mission. Even if he is aware of the prevailing military view on human life, the chaplain will not think of himself as being a bad military officer because he refuses to conform to that view. He will instead feel that the other military officers are wrong, that under the false claim of environmental necessity these officers have given approval to an attitude that is wrong regardless of the environment. The chaplain will believe that the other officers' attitudes—not his—should be changed. Thus the chaplain can even hold that his Christian attitudes represent the real best set of military attitudes as well. We have already seen that this point is well illustrated by the response of my chaplains to item 44 on the questionnaire for military chaplains. The respondents quite obviously felt that by upholding a Christian value of consideration for the life of the prisoners, they were also upholding the "true" values of the United States Army!

44. In almost every war there have been reports of soldiers being ordered to kill enemy prisoners. Had a chaplain been present when such orders were given, what should he have done?

___

___

___

___

Thus the chaplain is insulated to a certain degree from the causes of attitude change because he believes that Christian values are transcendental, thus relevant to any environment. To turn to the old military phrase, he can sincerely adopt the attitude that he is the only one in step. Of course if a chaplain's original religious values and the values of his military environment differed radically at every point, it would be extremely difficult for him to maintain a "transcendental" value stance; the chaplaincy would certainly be a role in tension. However, as we have pointed out (especially in Chapter 2), American Christianity and the American military themselves render a chaplain's "transcendental" value stance less threatening than it might otherwise be. As we have seen, the American church has often given credence to the claim that the United States (and her armed forces) is the hand of God, building his kingdom on earth. Furthermore, the United States Army, for its part, has frequently sought to embody many of the brightest American ideals. Indeed, the chaplain who attempts to halt the killing of prisoners in the name of the American military ethic has a secure base for his actions. Thus a chaplain's claim to be the only man in correct attitude step is rendered more plausible because the step of the regular troops is only slightly different.

In summary, then, I am arguing that *theories of attitude change do not explain variation in chaplain "militariness" because clergymen who become chaplains do not change their original clerical attitudes.* This argument has, in fact, been the main thrust of this entire study. Stated in this simple form, however, it leaves two important facts unexplained.

1. Undeniably, the attitudes of chaplains and of their civilian clergyman counterparts are extremely similar, but certain significant differences remain.
2. These attitudinal differences between clergymen and chaplains are not simply random; rather, they occur in connection with tasks and qualities over which clergyman and commander attitudes are most different (i.e., Hypothesis 1 appears to be borne out by the data).

In the remainder of this chapter I briefly suggest an explanation other than chaplain attitude change for the difference between the attitudes of chaplains and civilian clergymen.

Two factors, I believe, are of overriding importance in explaining these differences. The first should be obvious from the very nature of the Chaplain Corps. Clergymen, we must remember, are volunteers; they are not forced into the chaplaincy.[14] Such men do not enter the military "blind"; they know a good deal about the army—from reading, from personal observation (39% of my chaplain respondents had served in the armed forces before becoming clergymen and chaplains), from conversations with friends already in the chaplaincy. We would expect that the clergymen who entered the chaplaincy would be those who perceived a high degree of potential congruence between military and Christian values. Furthermore, if during his initial tour of duty the chaplain discovered irreconcilable differences between his attitudes and those prevalent in the military environment, he could refuse to extend his term of service. *It thus seems highly probable that self-selection into and defection out of the chaplaincy would account for at least some of the differences between the attitudes of chaplains and those of civilian clergymen.*

Besides this process of winnowing through self-selection and defection, there exists another explanation for the differences between chaplains and civilian clergymen, and I feel that it is at least equally important. The average chaplain has been in the army almost 10 years. *I* suggest that over those 10 years the chaplain's attitudes remained very much the same, whereas the attitudes of his civilian counterparts changed to a significant degree. It is not true that the military environment made the chaplain more "military"; instead, the military environment shielded him (at least in part) from forces that were making the civilian clergymen less military.

The synthesis between Christianity and Americanism was, of course, never quite so neat as I may have painted it in Chapter 2. There were always serious disjunctures between the word of God and the word of man. It seems, however, that only in the last decade have these disjunctures become visible to great numbers of American Christians. There are numerous reasons for this new awareness among American churchmen. Some reasons are theological—for example, the publication in 1918 (with numerous subsequent editions, only belatedly translated and brought to the United States) of Barth's *Romerbrief*.[15] Others were military and political—the doctrine of containment and the cold, bloody, inconclusive test it faced in Korea. Still others were economic— the depression of the 1930s, with its startling implications about the absolute "rightness" of our free enterprise system. However bringing the contradictions of Christ and American culture into sharp focus was probably accomplished by our 10-year war in Southeast Asia, especially the final period (1967-1972), which was accompanied by major protests at home. Religious protests to previous wars had been concentrated in the pacifist splinter denominations (which the American church as a whole tended to write off), but the situation in the late 1960s and early 1970s was different. Clergymen of all denominations went to jail because they could not reconcile the new demands of Caesar with the eternal claims of God. Not everyone agreed with the new criticism, of course, but its influence was great, and the changes it caused, if sometimes subtle, were frequently widespread:

> America's patriotic "civil religion," which Will Herberg in the mid-fifties had quite rightly designated as the basic faith of most Americans, was subjected to extremely severe criticism. The old nationalistic rhetoric was widely repudiated as hollow and deceitful. Nor did this civic faith die only in youthful hearts, for superannuated legislators were at the same time transforming the calendar of national holidays into a convenient series of long or lost weekends. On the other hand, there arose a veritable "great awakening" to the threat of environmental pollution and of the widespread depredations of nature which were robbing "America

the Beautiful" of its truth. Yet it was in connection with governmental priorities that sharpest conflict developed. Probably nothing did more to divest "The Star-Spangled Banner" of its unifying power than the subordination of social and economic needs to those of war and military might. Even flag-flying became a divisive symbol of the debates on law-and-order versus social justice.

In summary, one may safely say that America's moral and religious tradition was tested and found wanting in the sixties.[16]

Thus religion at home changed in the late 1960s and early 1970s. Yet during this period, religion within the military does not appear to have changed—or at least not in the same ways. Surely the problems facing a chaplain were different. But apparently the very nature and magnitude of these problems have prevented chaplains from grasping the deeper religious and theological implications. A chaplain, that is, can become so busy with successful drug abuse seminars (all aimed, in the best army tradition, at *isolating* the drug problem and *solving* it) that he does not have the time to analyze the harder question of whether there might have been a deep spiritual emptiness in soldiers fighting the Vietnam war—an emptiness that some soldiers sought to fill with drugs. Thus might the chaplain's very busyness with new problems prevent his seeing their deeper roots; thus might those problems isolate him still further from the religious value changes of the 1960s.[17]

The evidence is not conclusive in any formal manner, but I am nevertheless convinced that my primary point is valid: Over the past few years, "religion" for the civilian clergymen has changed; for the chaplains it has not.

I was not able to test this hypothesis directly from my data, but I have one set of findings that is suggestive. I decided to divide my civilian clergymen into two "generational" groups. The "older generation" (about 85% of my sample) was the set of clergymen who were ordained during or before 1966; the members of the "younger generation" (about 15%) were ordained in 1967 or more recently. The older generation, I assumed, would not have experienced so directly the great wave of social protest that swept the college campuses (including the seminaries) in the late 1960s and early 1970s. The younger generation of clergymen, on the other hand, should have had at least some contact with these forces. Thus I reasoned that although both generational groups had probably changed over the last few years, the younger generation might be expected to be in the forefront of the movement toward "new" religious values.

The reader should now recall the three old, familiar sets of attitudinal options on my questionnaires:

1. The 11 chaplain task options.
2. The five items that coded opinions on 1-to-5 scales.
3. The 14 qualities and personal belief options.

For each of these three sets I calculated the *total absolute differences* between the scores of the military commanders and the scores of (1) chaplains, (2) older-generation civilian clergymen, and (3) younger-generation civilian clergymen. My civilian religious change hypothesis suggested that total absolute differences between chaplains and commanders would be least, that differences between younger-generation clergymen and commanders would be greatest, and that differences between older-generation clergymen and commanders would lie somewhere in between. Table 7.1 presents the results of these calculations.

Table 7.1: Differences between Ratings by Military Commanders and by Three Clerical Groups

Item Set on Questionnaire	Differences between Ratings by Military Commanders and Ratings by the Following Groups:		
	Chaplains	Older-Generation Clergymen	Younger-Generation Clergymen
Tasks	29.1	30.2	45.4
"1-5" Questions	5.4	6.8	9.4
Qualities	47.5	53.5	55.4

Obviously the relationship is of the type we had expected; the younger-generation clergymen differ more from the military commanders (consequently from the chaplains) than do clergymen of the older generation. I see this finding as indicative of the shift in American religious values (noted by Ahlstrom and others) away from their historic congruence with the goals and means of American nationalism.

This chapter represents an attempt to demonstrate that attitudinal differences between chaplains and civilian clergymen are not the result of attitude change among chaplains but occur instead primarily because of a more general shift in religious values among civilian clergymen. Perhaps these attitudinal differences will soon disappear. After all, can we not expect the forces affecting civilian society eventually to reach into the army? And besides, the Chaplain Corps will soon be recruiting its members from among the "younger" generation of clergymen; surely these factors will bring chaplain and civilian clergyman attitudes back into more complete congruence!

This attitude divergence may be only temporary, but I doubt it. First, there seems to be a breakdown of communication between chaplains and those very clergymen (the less military ones) who could be the most important source of "new" religious values for the chaplains. I became aware of such a breakdown very early in my research. I had spent an extremely interesting evening talking to a very senior, rather conservative chaplain, who expressed concern that he no longer heard from an old friend, a fellow seminarian, now a well-known "radical" priest. Since the latter had long been a friend of mine too, I promised to bear a message. When I approached the other priest, his reply was to the point: "The only thing I could say to Chaplain X is that he should resign his commission, and he would not listen to that."[18] Thus was the fellowship broken.

This breakdown in communications was also obvious in many of my questionnaire returns. The younger clergymen, especially those who made the most cogent theological critique of the Vietnam war, were simply unwilling to talk about the matter with the chaplains, and their comments about their fellow clergymen in uniform sometimes bordered on vulgarity.

On the official, administrative level, this breakdown does not exist. Circulars and letters pour out from the endorsing agencies at an unprecedented rate. More retreats for chaplains and civilian clergymen are held than ever before. Yet this contact comes, for the most part, from the civilian clergymen whose attitudes are most like those of their brothers in the army, and this circumstance is not lost on the chaplains themselves. This is illustrated by the responses to item 22 on the questionnaire for military chaplains:

22. Do you feel that the civilian officials of your denomination show sufficient interest and concern for the needs and problems of the chaplaincy? _____

Quite a few chaplains contrasted official concern with lack of interest on the personal level. The words of a Methodist chaplain are perhaps representative:

The members of the Commission on Chaplains of the United Methodist Church are very concerned for the quality of ministry that is performed. However, I can not say that this is true for the Conference. It is the general consensus of local ministers that we chaplains have quit the ministry.[19]

Thus it seems that army chaplains tend to be isolated from the civilian clergymen who could be the very best source of dialogue and attitude change. Yet I do not feel that the overall attitude set of the Chaplain Corps will be greatly changed through the recruitment of the younger, less military clergymen. This somewhat pessimistic conclusion was suggested by an examination of chaplain responses to my survey. Although most chaplains do not enter the army immediately following ordination,[20] a number of respondents (less than 10%) fall into the "younger generation" as we defined it for the civilian clergymen (those ordained in or after 1967). And whereas most "younger generation" civilian clergymen were much less military than their "older" colleagues, this pattern did not hold true for the chaplains. Apparently the process of chaplain self-selection now works to exclude the "new breed" of younger clergymen, for there is virtually no difference in attitude between chaplains of the "younger" and "older" generations.[21]

In conclusion, I have tried to show that the attitudinal differences between chaplains and civilian clergymen have resulted from a value shift among the clergymen. I have further suggested that this new divergence is not a temporary phenomenon. One final question remains: What is the possible significance of these chaplain-clergyman differences for the Chaplain Corps, for the army, for the American church as a whole? This question is the subject of the final chapter of this study.

NOTES

1. Environmental difference scores and attitudinal adaptation scores were calculated for each option as follows. The mean rating of the military commanders was subtracted from the mean rating of the civilian clergyman to yield a number A. The mean rating of the military chaplains was subtracted from the mean rating of the civilian clergymen to yield a number B.

Environmental difference scores were always positive numbers equal to the absolute value of A.

Attitudinal adaptation scores were equal in absolute magnitude to B; their signs were determined as follows: If A and B had like signs, the sign of the adaptation score was positive; otherwise it was negative.

Thus the environmental difference scores are positive numbers giving for each option the magnitude of the difference between clergyman and commander ratings. The attitudinal adaptation scores give the difference between clergyman and chaplain ratings. Usually these latter scores are positive—except when the chaplains are less "military" than the civilian clergymen, in which case the attitudinal adaptation scores are negative.

To lessen the degree of heteroscedasticity, options marked with an "X" were given a code value of 12 rather than the 20-value assigned in a previous chapter. This coding difference did not noticeably change orders of importance ratings.

2. The mean legitimacy scores were subtracted, not added, because with them lower values indicate greater "militariness."

3. Rank was coded as follows: captain = 2, major = 3, lieutenant colonel = 4, colonel = 5, brigadier general = 6, major general = 7. Service schools were counted as follows: One point was given for each service school attended, but the following schools received higher point values as indicated: war colleges, 3 points; Command and General Staff College, Industrial College of the Armed Forces, 2 points. Each chaplain received a score equal to the total points for all the service schools he had attended.

4. Weekly communication was coded as "4"; monthly contact was coded as "3"; communication only a "couple of times" a year was coded as "2"; still less frequent communication was coded as "1."

5. The variable friends was taken from item 23 on the questionnaire for military chaplains. An option within the question, when checked, was given a code value as indicated below:

    23. Of your personal friends who are also fellow clergymen,

       1 virtually all are military chaplains
       2 most are chaplains, but a few are civilian clergymen
       3 about half are chaplains; about half are civilian clergymen
       4 most are civilian clergymen, but a few are military chaplains
       5 virtually all are civilian clergymen.

6. More specifically, the model was stated as follows: overall militariness =

$$a + b_1 x_1 + b_2 x_2 + b_3 x_3 + b_4 x_4 + b_5 x_5 + b_6 x_6 + b_7 x_7 + b_8 x_8 + b_9 x_9 + b_{10} x_{10}$$

where x_1 = years service x_6 = study
          x_2 = rank x_7 = prayer
          x_3 = combat x_8 = civilian preaching
          x_4 = service schools x_9 = communication
          x_5 = periodicals x_{10} = friends

7. When the number of observations is as large as that in the present sample, regression coefficients without statistical significance virtually never have any theoretical or practical significance.

8. George Homans, *The Human Group*, p. 144.

9. More specifically, the model was stated as follows:

$$\text{militariness} = a + b_1 x_1 + b_2 x_2 + b_3 x_3 + b_4 x_4 + b_5 x_5 + b_6 x_6$$

where x_1 = rank
x_2 = medals
x_3 = campaigns
x_4 = importance
x_5 = expected enlisted rating
x_6 = expected commander rating

10. The coefficients for variables medals, expected enlisted rating, and expected commander rating were without statistical significance, taken singly or in any combination. Taken together, the variables rank and importance were barely significant in adding to the total explained sum of squares, but since it is not possible to state with any certainty even the signs of their coefficients, and since neither is statistically significant when taken alone, it is not necessary to discuss them in the body of the text. However, these two variables are included in a general model, discussed shortly.

11. More specifically, the model was stated as follows:

$$\text{militariness} = a + b_1x_1 + b_2x_2 + b_3x_3 + b_4x_4 + b_5x_5$$

where x_1 = years service
x_2 = study
x_3 = campaigns
x_4 = rank
x_5 = importance

12. The regression equation for the combined model is

$$\text{overall militariness} = -8.59 + 0.65x_1 + 2.63x_3 - 2.63x_4 + 1.54x_5$$

where x_1 = years service
x_2 = study (not significant, therefore not included)
x_3 = campaigns
x_4 = rank
x_5 = importance

13. And I have omitted even the mention of about 20 more whose connection with "militariness," it turned out, was too remote to bear reporting. The statistically sophisticated reader might also ask at this point how "significant" a couple of variables with $p = c\ .05$ are when nearly 40 variables and variable combinations have been tested.

14. There are a very few semiexceptions to this rule. Up until 1968, rabbis (who are not included in this study) were occasionally "drafted" by their denomination for service in the armed forces. Similarly, a small number of Roman Catholic priests are apparently pressured by their ecclesiastical superiors to join the chaplaincy, which is always a bit short of Catholic pastors.

15. Karl Barth's celebrated commentary on Paul's epistle to the Romans had come, it was said, like the tolling of a great bell on the continental theological scene. Barth emphasized that the word of God is radically transcendent, that it comes upon man "at right angles from above" *(senkrecht, von oben).* Thus within the framework of Barthian theology, one could speak only with extreme caution of any unity of divine and national purposes.

16. Sydney E. Ahlstrom, *A Religious History of the American People,* p. 1085.

17. In two articles for the *Atlanta Journal* and the *Atlanta Constitution*, Bill Montgomery and B. C. Speed suggest that chaplains now have so many specific problem-solving roles that they consider "religion" only a small part of their business. One of my respondents (a Catholic captain) sees the problem somewhat differently: "In point of fact the vast majority of troops have extremely little to do with religion or a religious minister. To keep busy chaplains now specialize in anything." At any rate it appears that some chaplains may manage to keep so busy in their new-found tasks that they do not notice the depth of the changes that have been taking place in American religion and society.

18. The exact circumstances, as well as the words of the priest's reply, have been slightly altered to preserve the anonymity of the participants.

19. A Methodist major.

20. The average chaplain has been ordained for 6.2 years before he enters military service.

21. It appears, in other words, that not so many years ago a civilian clergyman picked at random from any of the mainline American denominations probably would have held about the same religious values and opinions as the average chaplain. Under such conditions it would not have been very meaningful to talk about the self-selection of clergymen into the chaplaincy. Over time, however, the religious values of civilian clergymen have apparently "liberalized," while chaplains' values have remained about the same (or at least have not kept up with the civilian "liberalizing" trends). Under the present conditions, self-selection of chaplains is becoming increasingly important in enabling the army to continue to recruit about the same "type" of chaplain.

Chapter 8

FURTHER REFLECTIONS AND CONCLUSION

The spirit of West Point is in the great, gray, Gothic Chapel, starting from the hill and dominating The Plain, calling to mind Henry Adams' remarks at Mont St. Michel on the unity of the military and the religious spirits.
Samuel Huntington

A peace-preaching chaplain named Wiley
Was told by the Colonel, quite slyly,
"I can't make you cease,
But if your pants lack a crease
I swear you'll be jailed at Fort Riley!"
Benning Limericks

There is a sense in which this study is now finished. Its purpose has been introduced, its methodology has been explained, and its findings have been presented and analyzed. I am not ready to give it up yet, however, for I firmly believe that at some point every serious researcher must extricate himself from the immediacy of his data and ask himself (still in the light of these data), "So what?"

With regard to values I hold important, my findings leave me with a feeling of optimism. There is optimism because our army, more than most other military forces, including many it has had for allies and enemies during this century, attempts to preserve respect for human life and dignity. There is optimism because the Chaplain Corps has remained remarkably faithful to the original source of its religious attitudes, even within the sometimes contradictory military environment. There is optimism because civilian clergymen (indeed the American church generally) seem to be increasingly less willing to accept a nationalistic definition of Christianity. I should like to dwell awhile in the optimism, then bring my essay to a quick close, forgetting for now the darker side of the picture. And yet it is to this less happy business that we should direct our fullest attention; it is, after all, in darkness that light is most useful.

If I am correct, the divergence between the attitudes of chaplains and clergymen[1] is but one manifestation of a larger political (and theological) problem. In an earlier work, Major Raoul H. Alcala and I used techniques of quantitative analysis to demonstrate that in many ways, the content of various military journals and army service schools was becoming more overtly political.[2] We had originally suspected that this reflected politicizing changes occurring throughout all the American professions, civilian as well as military. A later paper, however, shows that such is not the case; instead, this area seems to yield examples of a growing difference between the army and American society as a whole.[3]

More directly to the point is the work of Samuel Huntington. In *The Soldier and the State* he makes a complicated and rather effective argument that the loyalty of an army can be guaranteed only when the organization is founded on the norms of apolitical professionalism, when its officers and administrators remain clear of the political process. Huntington further argues that an apolitical, professional military force can remain strong only when there is a basic congruence between the values of military professionalism and those of civilian society. That is the professional military officer is basically conservative. He takes a worst-case view of international relations, and thus wants always to possess sufficient military power to defeat any enemy. If the segment of government that authorizes military expenditures is also of this conservative mind, the army will be maintained at what the military officer considers adequate strength. If, however, the governmental authority is imbued with a more optimistic, "liberal" philosophy, insufficient men and material (at least according to the military officer's way of thinking) will be forthcoming, and the military officer will be faced with a choice: either see the military forces maintained at an "inadequate" level or enter the political process to ensure a force of "adequate" strength.

None of this, Huntington felt, had caused any serious problem in America until the mid-twentieth century, when the United States was first faced with a powerful, external security threat. After that, tension developed. Furthermore, Huntington felt that "The tension between the demands of military security and the values of American liberalism can, in the long run, be relieved only by the weakening of the security threat or the weakening of liberalism."[4] Since Huntington did not consider the security threat to be a variable that was subject to manipulation, he was willing to call for the weakening of liberalism as a means of reducing the tension.[5]

Further Reflections and Conclusion

Our analysis of the chaplaincy follows in some ways Huntington's analysis of the military ethic and liberalism. Historically American chaplains have been able without tension to serve two masters because both masters appeared to want much the same thing. Today, however, there is an increasing divergence between religion as the military would have it defined and Christianity as the churches do in fact define it. The day will come, I feel, when the contrast that Huntington feared between the American military ethic and the American civilian ethic[6] will be nowhere greater than in the field of religion. And the chaplain will be left, straddling the gap that has become a chasm! The church, of course, cannot seek to avoid that day of trial; she must follow as well as she can the will of her Master and not seek to hold her values in Huntingtonian congruence with the military ethic. Nevertheless, forewarned of the storm that may someday break, churchmen should think out clearly what a chaplain should be if he is to render greatest service to the army and the nation while remaining faithful to the Shepherd and his sheep.

There are at least two ways of approaching the problem of defining the chaplain's proper position within the complex matrix of church-state relations. If we begin with a more or less concrete notion of the "ideal" relationship of religion to the state, we could seek to define for the chaplaincy an organizational structure that would reflect the principles of that relationship. Methodologically, such an approach has considerable initial appeal. We would decide on a goal, then construct the means for its realization. This method has recently been applied by many who subscribe to the "Christ against culture" position,[7] feeling that elements of antimilitariness and conflict should be part of the very structure of the chaplaincy.[8] Also—and this should not be so very surprising—the same mode of analysis has been utilized by people who are convinced that the church should be in constant harmony with the state. Such individuals are quite willing to structure the chaplaincy to allow it to legitimate the goals and missions of the armed forces.

The very latitude with which this "define the relationship and build a structure" method has been applied clearly illustrates the strength of its appeal. It can also indicate, however, the inadequacy of such an approach: Those who utilize it commit themselves to the view that the relationship of church to state is static. If one builds antimilitariness into the chaplaincy, creating opportunities for conflict, it will become difficult for the chaplain ever to exhort the troops toward victory, even for the liberation of an Auschwitz. On the other hand, if one structures the chaplaincy as an institutional affirmation of the oneness of church and state, he can scarcely expect the chaplain to stand against military policies, even when they lead to a My Lai. In either case, practically speaking, one limits the flexibility of the chaplaincy; theologically speaking, one denies the *potentia Dei absoluta.*

The alternative way to define a proper chaplaincy is to address the problem from a particular theological base. This approach, too, is fraught with perils, and the most important is quite adequately illustrated by the works of Zahn, Burchard, et al. The basic error occurs when (1) a theological definition is posited for Christianity *and* (2) the chaplains who are discovered (by social science techniques) to deviate from that definition are assumed to have changed their attitudes or sold out their convictions. This mistake, at least, I must continue to avoid.

It is possible, of course, to question the propriety of a social scientist's dealing with theological definitions at all. Nevertheless, I feel compelled to say something about what the chaplaincy can and should be in America today. I also believe that the reshaping of theology to meet temporal "needs" borders on heresy. Therefore I shall offer a rough theological definition of the ideal chaplaincy. *Then* we can consider the secular advantages—political and otherwise—that may be derived from it.

It is quite impossible to have any real theological sense of what a chaplain should be without a firm understanding of the church's mission in the world. That mission itself has been the subject of increasing discussion, and it is not feasible to present even the briefest outline of the debate. Before we can proceed to discuss the chaplaincy, however, I must lay out the framework of my ideas on the church's mission.

For perhaps a century a hymn called "There Is a Balm in Gilead" has been very popular among the churches of the rural South. One of its verses runs like this:

> If you can't preach like Peter,
> If you can't pray like Paul,
> Just tell the love of Jesus
> And say he died for all!

This old hymn quite succinctly sums up the church's mission—to witness to the saving power of God's love in the world. The priestly proclamation of grace (through word and sacrament) is obviously a primary task of the church. The mission, however, must not cease

Further Reflections and Conclusion

there; the preaching of God's love will seem a ministry of empty words unless those words are accompanied by the pastoral practice of grace — the helping of others. Finally, a real Christian witness must affirm that God's love manifested itself not only in the crucifixion but also in the resurrection. If grace is victorious, the church must proclaim as prophet that the kingdom of God is truly at hand. Of the church's three missions, the task of prophecy is probably the most difficult to understand. Since it is also a primary political importance, however, we must examine it in some detail. First of all, the prophecy of the kingdom is complex; it is almost paradoxical. Man cannot bring in the kingdom through his own deeds; it is realized by God alone, through his unaided efforts, in his own time. And yet the action of man is not unimportant. The church universal has been given grace to recognize the signs of the kingdom, and she must point them out to humankind. Also, and this has sometimes been even more important, the church has grace to see what things are *not* signs of the kingdom. Patently, no creation of man that claims to be an absolute, final answer to the questions of meaning and existence can be a part of God's kingdom. During the twentieth century such claims of ultimacy have manifested themselves most frequently in the political realm. Furthermore, these claims, even when based on the highest and most noble of principles, have seldom been without disastrous consequences. (Hence Stalin's Russia with its supposed foundation of high Marxist idealism became perverted and is remembered with little more affection than Hitler's Germany and its base of blood and race.) It is the prophetic task of the church to stand firmly against all political claims of ultimacy, and it is especially the mission of the church to oppose such claims when they tend to divide people by classes, sexes, races, or ethnic groups. Thus for the prophetic church, the status of the state must remain somewhat ambiguous. On the one hand, the state can transcend the older cleavages that split mankind; on the other hand, the state draws new, sometimes deeper lines of separation across the brotherhood of humanity. Also, the modern nation-state tends to claim that the benefits (real and chimerical) it provides to its citizens are the fruits of some particular ideology. Frequently this ideology, together with the nation's goals, its techniques, and its organs of execution, is further assumed to lend the country a status of sacral untouchability. One result of this is the possibility of "holy" war in defense of ideology. Here the church that confesses God's transcendent kingdom must proclaim that a war can never be *just* simply because it is fought for Communism or Freedom (or presumably for anything else that begins with a capital letter, including especially Christianity).[9]

The church's witness to God's love must also be the mission of the chaplain. All three elements of the proclamation (priestly, pastoral, and prophetic) must be present, for the absence of even one renders the other two incomplete. In seeking to develop a Christian chaplaincy, the church must eventually ask what structural forms are best suited to the fulfillment of the threefold ministry that has been theologically defined.

In the past, the church has apparently viewed the chaplaincy according to an extremely literal interpretation of Jesus' commission to *preach* the gospel (Mark 3, Luke 9). Getting the word and sacraments to the soldiers was given the highest religious priority. And for this purpose the chaplaincy as it had evolved seemed to be admirably suited. It was certainly convenient for the civilian denominations; the army paid the preachers and provided them with everything necessary, from transportation to pulpits and communion sets (air-droppable, with olive-drab cases). The setup also ensured that every soldier would have the priestly service of a chaplain readily available. It is not clear, however, that the current administrative structure of the chaplaincy is quite so conducive to the performance of pastoral and prophetic roles. Here the question of a chaplain's military status is salient. It was comparatively recently that the system of chaplain ranks and promotion became a part of general army policy,[10] and over the years there has been extensive debate on the question of rank for chaplains. Unfortunately, I did not probe this question in my questionnaires; I had been informed that most chaplains were tired of the discussion and that to include a question directly relevant to it would seriously lower my return rates. Nevertheless, I did include one item that was indirectly related to chaplain's rank and officer-status:

Do you ever feel a serious conflict of values because of the dual nature of your clergyman-officer role? _____

The great majority of the chaplains (almost 90%) said they never felt any value conflict. A number of these, however, went on to say that to avoid such conflict it was occasionally necessary to de-emphasize one's role as an officer. (No chaplain responded that he de-emphasized his role as clergyman.) The following responses are perhaps representative:

No. I regard myself as a priest.[11]
No. I ignore the officer role as much as possible.[12]
No. I think I'm a poor officer.[13]

Further Reflections and Conclusion

In addition, a number of chaplains wrote extensive extra comments that bear directly on the matter of rank and officer status. Some felt that their rank and officer status were definite assets: "Being officers opens doors which would be closed otherwise,"[14] and "Rank helps some S.O.B. to listen!"[15]

On the other hand, a somewhat larger number of chaplains questioned the propriety of a clergyman's holding rank and bearing a military commission. Roughly speaking, these comments fell into two categories. Some were concerned that a chaplain's rank and officer status might hinder his communication with enlisted men, thus interfere with his pastoral ministry:

> I personally think that a chaplain should not wear rank. . . . Too many chaplains have become rank-conscious, which is detrimental to their day-to-day dealings with the soul of the young soldier.[16]
>
> Being an officer really is a built-in barrier to the E.M.[17]

Others are more concerned that rank and officer status tend to negate the possibilities of a prophetic ministry. One chaplain asked, somewhat rhetorically,

> Where was the chaplain at My Lai?
> Why didn't he have the balls to solve that problem then and there?
> Why [do] chaplains . . . worry about their Efficiency Report and become yes-men to the commander?
> Why must the chaplain have rank?[18]

And another chaplain more gently asks about "the paradox of wearing a cross on one's lapel and a military insignia [of rank] on the other—can and should a clergyman ever be comfortable in that situation?"[19]

There are, then, at least some chaplains who feel that the current rank structure is not without drawbacks. (And indeed, even those who are impressed with the advantages of rank could be just a bit dissatisfied. At present the chaplain has only rank, with no authority to command. Perhaps a chaplain with authority as well as rank would find that rank accomplished more than "help some S.O.B. to listen" to his prophetic words; it could *make* him listen!) Therefore, I feel strongly that both the church and the army should examine closely the current rank structure and consider the possibility of change. I have no detailed program, but it might be helpful to try an adaptation of the British navy solution.[20] Clergymen could be appointed to the pay grade of chaplain. Within that pay grade there could be various subdivisions (corresponding perhaps to the GS system) which would not be indicated by any badge on the chaplain's uniform. The chaplain would be given no specific rank, but according to the law he would assume temporarily the rank of the person to whom he was talking. In good Pauline fashion he could be a general to generals, to privates a private (see I Corinthians 9:22). If this scheme were not thought practical, the army might consider (on an experimental basis) the appointment of a few noncommissioned chaplains (say as SP/5s) or even a no-rank chaplaincy.

By these or some other schemes, the bars that rank presents to communication might be lowered or eliminated. The problem of aiding the chaplain's prophetic ministry, however, is of a different order. Here it is doubtful that any structural changes the army might make could be of any real value. These changes, like the message of prophecy itself, must be initiated from outside the military environment. Several partial remedies suggest themselves. Up until 1968 at least a certain percentage of Jewish chaplains were "drafted" by their civilian religious leaders. The rationale behind this "draft" was twofold. On the one hand, these leaders felt, as long as the armed forces included Jewish personnel, these personnel had to be supplied with the ministry of ordained rabbis. On the other hand, it was assumed that the "drafting" of seminary graduates would bypass the normal self-selection process of becoming a chaplain. Thus there would be in the armed forces some rabbis who did not fit precisely into the military mold, and perhaps a few who were actively antimilitary. It was hoped by the "drafting" procedure to keep alive within the military the strong tradition of an independent Jewish prophetic ministry.[21]

This practice of "drafting" rabbis has now ceased, but perhaps the principle behind it was not in error; it is certain that much of the most vigorous in-house criticism of the army and the Chaplain Corps has come from Jewish chaplains and from rabbis who had been chaplains.[22] Similarly, among my respondents a few Catholic priests give pressure from their ecclesiastical superiors as their primary reason for joining the chaplaincy. In general, these priests are significantly less "military" than their colleagues. For the Roman Catholic and United Methodist churches (whose clergymen are subject to the discipline of church bishops), it would be administratively a simple matter to institute a chaplain draft. Furthermore, the church endorsing agencies could promise to protect their chaplains from any military prosecution that might result from conscientious opposition to military policy.[23] In addition, civilian ministers and priests concerned with the lack of prophetic ministry within the chaplaincy should be encouraged to volunteer their own services. If not too old, they could become chaplains; better still, they could volunteer as medics or even infantrymen and carry out their ministry in an informal, military worker-priest context. Still more important, and I feel that this is a minimum Christian demand, the more "radical" civilian clergymen must attempt to keep open lines of communication to personnel who are already serving in the chaplaincy. These clergymen must promise the chaplains their support through fellowship and prayer, and they must exhort the chaplains not to neglect their prophetic duties.[24] Most important of all, the Christian laity within the military, officers and enlisted men alike, should remember that the prophetic message of God's love must and will be spoken. If the chaplains sometimes fail to preach it in full force, that does not mean that any other Christian is thereby excused from the duty of proclamation.

The theologian, of course, need look no further than his definition of mission to argue that the ministry of prophecy must receive its proper emphasis within the chaplaincy (and indeed within the American church as a whole, where it has frequently been neglected). As a political scientist, however, I suggest that the development of a prophetic ministry within the military could have as a by-product a highly beneficial effect for the nation and its armed forces.

For the country as a whole this advantage will be in the area of organizational control. Overall, current trends toward the separation of the military from society seem most likely to continue.[25] The military services will recruit their enlisted personnel from a more limited spectrum of society than has formerly been the case. The cessation of the draft, which ended the induction (limited though it had always been) of well-educated, liberal young men into the army, also removed a major impetus for this type of person to join the other services.[26] Sources of officer recruitment will be even more seriously narrowed. Though the all-volunteer army necessarily will be smaller than our previous forces, with fewer officer positions to be filled, the service academies have recently been substantially enlarged.[27] Short-time ROTC officers, with their nonmilitary value orientations, will no longer be in great demand,[28] for West Pointers (socialized into the military environment throughout their more specialized education) will be able to fill an increasing number of the lieutenants' slots, particularly in the crucial combat arms. Within the ROTC program itself, significant changes are also taking place. In just three years (1968-1971) cadet enrollments had dropped by more than 60%, from 218,466 to 87,807.[29] Part of this decline was caused by individual decisions to avoid military service completely. Perhaps an even more significant factor has been the removal of ROTC units from many of the nation's college campuses. As even the casual observer knows, the army's loss of ROTC units has not been randomly spread across all American colleges; it has instead been concentrated among the leading universities—schools that used to provide a high proportion of the nation's leaders in all fields. According to Charles Moskos,

> The ROTC units from which the bulk of the officer corps is now drawn will almost certainly decrease in number and narrow in range. Partly as a result of anti-ROTC agitation at prestige colleges and universities, ROTC recruitment will be increasingly found in educational institutions located in regions where the status of the military profession is highest—rural areas and in the South and mountain states. It must be candidly acknowledged that such ROTC units will often be at colleges and universities with modest academic standards.[30]

It should be clear, then, that in the competition for high-ranking positions West Point graduates will possess increasing advantages (militarily, since they will have held the more prestigious junior officer positions; educationally, at least frequently, because the "best" civilian colleges have long since axed their ROTC programs). It is not yet completely clear what political significance this general narrowing of recruitment bases may have, but some have seen it as inappropriate for (and perhaps even dangerous to) a democratic society:

> Under a volunteer system service academy graduates will achieve an even stronger hold on the higher echelons of the military. The mix of the past will be eliminated.... America will draw its military leaders from a narrow, inbred group, not as well educated, not coming from a broad cross section of American higher educational institutions, and not as close to the mainstream of its democratic institutions. Thus, there will arise an isolated elite in the officer corps at the top and an equally isolated group, socially and economically in the enlisted ranks below. Such a military can hardly be viewed as a solid foundation for a democratic society.[31]

Cutbacks in the number of army personnel are also making it possible for an increasing percentage of soldiers and soldiers' families to live on post, and the rising cost of living has made post exchange and commissary facilities effective drawing cards indeed. Furthermore, this development has been encouraged by the efforts of post commanders to make their installations more attractive places to spend leisure time. In at least some cases this has been done in the conscious attempt to separate military personnel from a civilian society that is seen as the source of many drug, race, and discipline problems.[32]

All these factors of selective recruitment and separated housing appear to indicate a return to the isolation from society that characterized the American army from 1876 until World War II.[33] According to Samuel Huntington, it was precisely this isolation, together with the absence of any serious threat to America's military security, that led to the formation of the conservative military ethic. Huntington, of course, praised the spirit of professionalism that developed from this first separation of army and society.[34] As we have seen, however, he was fearful that a near-total separation of military and civilian values, *when accompanied by the perception within the military of serious threats to national security*, would prove dangerous to the principles of civilian control over the military.[35] Such, according to John S. Ambler, was the case with the French army in Algeria. Forced to fight one unpopular war on the heels of another, and deprived as they saw it of moral and material support at home, the highly professional officers of the French airborne battalions felt spiritually isolated from the very country they were sworn to defend. Eventually these officers came to believe that the "liberal" civilian leaders of France were no longer taking steps adequate to the defense of the homeland. And the paratroop commanders entered the political arena quite dramatically.[36]

We should certainly not suggest that the United States Army of the future will come to resemble the mutinous French army of the late 1950s and early 1960s. In certain ways, however, our army has increasingly involved itself in the domestic and political affairs of the United States. The surveillance of civilian politicians by the military intelligence services and the employment of federal troops in the control of civil disturbances are only the most dramatic examples. The lobbying of Defense Department personnel before Congress and the involvement of the armed forces in domestic civic action projects may be equally important.

The coupling of the army's increased political action with its increased ideological estrangement could put unprecedented strains on the American system of civil-military relations. Here the value of a prophetic Christian ministry would be beyond question. The chaplain could bring to the army a message that came from outside the military attitude complex. The prophetic chaplain, while *in* the army, could never be completely *of* the army. Neither could he be identified as an "agent" of alien civilian influences, for his message would transcend the ideology of civilian society as much as it would that of the military. And although the Christian church does not presently appear likely to overcome her internal divisions, a united, prophetic church and chaplaincy might help bridge any gap developing between the military and American society, by transcending both.

Besides this general advantage to the American nation as a whole, a prophetic chaplain could also directly benefit the Army itself in an area of utmost importance,[37] namely, the widely decried erosion of military integrity. It is certainly not the purpose of this book to offer any catalogue of military dishonor. There are published accounts of our army's involvement in illegal and immoral activities that range from the killing of Vietnamese civilians to slot-machine corruption and the smuggling of orangutans.[38] The army has been "exposed" too often for the sake of mere exposure. We should remember that the true prophets of old chastised Israel not from hatred but because they loved her. *Nevertheless, they did demand repentance; they did command in God's name that Israel turn from her wickedness, corporate as well as individual!* Thus the prophetic chaplain is concerned with sin.

The theologian, of course, would eventually diagnose the basic sin of our army and its personnel as the timeless human root weakness of wanting to be God. On the organizational level, our army has considered its mission as supremely important, as justifying anything. At the individual level, some officers have given their own careers within the military an importance that has led to moral compromise.

There is, I feel, a direct connection between the army's egotistical sense of self-importance (which the theologian defines as sin) and the erosion of military integrity (which so many critics have noted in the closing years of the Vietnam decade). Few men have understood this connection better than a certain West Point professor who has chosen, despite the contradictions, to stick it out on active duty. In speaking of today's army, Major James S. Dickey writes:

> The drive for mission accomplishment and winning runs deep. There may be reason for not accomplishing a mission but never an excuse. Not accomplishing a mission is failure. Therefore, from the beginning of an officer's career, the army is checking him against a standard of accomplishing missions, preferably in spite

Further Reflections and Conclusion [147]

of circumstances which would favor failure. From "pass that inspection" to "take that hill" to "win in Vietnam," the only criterion is favorable results. With winning the only standard, the imperatives of honor start to erode.[39]

Dickey then relates how false paperwork is completed to "cover" inspections, how overly optimistic intelligence forecasts are given—all to make it seem that the precious mission is being accomplished when, quite often, the reverse is true.[40] The effects of this practice are nowhere more clearly illustrated than in the Hamlet Evaluation Program in Vietnam. Carl Thayer has shown an interesting pattern that frequently repeated itself when a new officer was assigned duties related to hamlet security and evaluation. Newly arrived officers frequently tended to rate most of the hamlets within their districts as quite insecure. Toward the end of their respective tours, the hamlets were rated as more secure; thus an officer could show "improvement" under his direction. When a new officer was assigned to replace the original rater, however, the pattern tended to recur. The same hamlets were rated insecure, only to become "more secure" toward the tour's end.[41] Similarly, the research of Richard Rinaldi indicates that even the Agency for International Development, with its notoriously overoptimistic reports, tended to give a more sober, accurate account of the situation in Vietnam than did the army.[42]

Somewhat paradoxically, then, a situation had arisen in which the prophetic chaplain would have no more important mission than to speak for a renewed emphasis on the old *military* virtue of integrity within our army. That the chaplain did not always understand the relationship of a prophetic ministry to the deterioration of military honor is illustrated by the aftermath of My Lai. In the days that followed the tragic operation, the picture of what had happened became increasingly clear at the 23rd Infantry ("Americal") Division Headquarters in Chu Lai.[43] The division chaplain eventually got wind of the occurrence, and when he learned that numerous women and children had been killed, he was quoted as follows: "Gee, who in the world goofed on this? Who in the world goofed?"[44]

I shall not contend that a prophetic chaplaincy would immediately remedy all the darker ills of today's army, but I do feel quite strongly that the voice of godly prophecy speaks directly to the basic question of integrity. The word of God is a constant reminder that the accomplishment of the mission does not automatically justify the application of any means.[45] The word of God is a constant reminder that we human beings, made whole and just by Christ's love, are of too much worth to sacrifice our integrity for earthly praise and paltry institutional advancement. The word of God is a constant reminder that in the West Point motto, honor is just as important as duty or country!

CONCLUSION

This book was begun under the tacit assumption that the chaplaincy was used in a rather straightforward way to legitimate the goals and missions of the United States Army. During the course of my research, however, I became convinced that such is not the case. It is certain that the maintenance of this independence from the demands of the military environment has required persistent dedication, courage, and even sacrifice on the part of the chaplains themselves. In the light of this quiet, steadfast heroism, it may be improper for one outside the ministry to ask for more, to say that the chaplain must stand ever prepared to belabor a human, erring army with prophetic criticism. Nevertheless, I think the time has come for the words of prophecy to be said. I am also convinced that the chaplain will find the strength to say them; after all, he is not operating alone:

> To be a Christian minister in the world in 1972 is a difficult moral struggle. To be ordained at all by the church is AGONY, yet it is with hope and trust that I and others work for the recovery of broken relationships. Wholeness in personal relationships is what I seek through the instrument of Christ's Church. HE WILL ULTIMATELY ACCOMPLISH THAT![46]

NOTES

1. Note that according to the preceding chapter, this divergence is both recent in origin and increasing in size.
2. Clarence L. Abercrombie, III, and Major Raoul H. Alcalá, U.S. Army. "The New Military Professionalism," in *Military Force and American Society,* Bruce M. Russett and Alfred Stepan (Eds.).
3. Abercrombie, "Politicization."
4. Samuel Huntington. *The Soldier and the State,* p. 456.
5. Ibid., p. 464.
6. Recent research by Norman Nie ("Mass Belief Systems Revisited," *Journal of Politics,* 36, 3 (August, 1974), pp. 540-91, convincingly documents a new polarization in the American political arena. During the 1950s political scientists

Further Reflections and Conclusion [149]

had discovered that many American voters held a "conservative" opinion on one issue and a "liberal" opinion on another. Thus it was impossible to divide the American public along any general ideological line. Nie finds, however, that since the early 1960s conservative opinions on one issue have become correlated with conservative opinions on other (even nonrelated) issues. (The same holds for liberal issues, naturally.) Thus it is possible, for the first time in recent years, to think in terms of an ideological split in American politics. (See Nie, especially pp. 9, 11 and Figs. 1 and 2.) Nie's work is basically concerned with demonstrating that there has indeed been a polarization in American politics, and Nie does not attempt to specify the demographic compositions of the poles themselves; he does not try to say what kinds of people are on which side of the liberal-conservative split. Nevertheless, whether the split is between the military and civilian society or (as seems more likely) within civilian society, with the military aligned with the conservatives and the church becoming increasingly aligned with the liberals, the position of the chaplain seems certain to become more critical in the years ahead.

7. See H. Richard Niebuhr, *Christ and Culture*.

8. Ralph Weltge, "The Greening of the Military Chaplaincy." It also appears that the United Church of Christ may by leaning toward this view; see *Ministries to Military Personnel*.

9. When thinking of the prophetic ministry, it may be helpful to consider the church in two modes, as a religious *institution* and as a religious *movement*. This dichotomy is strongly emphasized in the Old Testament and certainly continues today. Politically prophetic criticism is generally most powerful where the institutional church becomes enlivened by the church-as-movement, so that both speak with one voice. Such a situation may now be developing, for example, in Brazil, where the institutional church has occasionally regarded the political regime as a real adversary (see Luigi Einaudi et al., *Latin American Institutional Development*, pp. 47-48, and "Onward Christian Soldiers."

On the other hand, in the United States the institutional church (at least according to most statistical indicators) has flourished as perhaps nowhere else on earth, and most of the politically prophetic criticism has come not from the church-as-institution but rather from the church-as-movement. Furthermore, the development of prophetic currents within American Christianity has been greatly hindered by the general poverty of American theological thought since the death of Jonathan Edwards. In fact, I suggest that since the days of Timothy Dwight and the development of the so-called *theologica gloria*, American churchmen have not been even interested in theological studies. The church-as-movement was too busy; the church-as-institution was too self-satisfied.

10. For instance, at the beginning of the War Between the States, Union chaplains were appointed in the grade of private. See Sydney E. Ahlstrom, *A Religious History of the American People*, pp. 674-676.

11. A Catholic colonel.
12. A Catholic captain.
13. A Catholic captain.
14. A Southern Baptist captain.
15. A Lutheran major.
16. A Catholic captain.
17. A Southern Baptist major.

18. A United Methodist major.
19. A Catholic captain.
20. The British navy chaplain is given no specific rank; instead, he addresses each person as if his own rank were equivalent to the rank of the other person.
21. This information was gathered from private conversations with Chaplain (CPT) Mark Weiner, U.S.A., a rabbi who is currently a graduate student in Yale University's Department of Sociology. Chaplain Weiner suggests that this reasoning may have been in part an ex post facto rationalization for the necessity of a draft.
22. See, for example, the article by Rabbi Martin Siegel and Bruce M. Freyer in Harvey G. Cox (ed.), *Military Chaplains*.
23. In general, persons released from the military cannot be tried under the Uniform Code of Military Justice. When a religious denomination withdraws the endorsement of a chaplain, he must immediately be released from active duty. Of course in some cases a released chaplain would be subject to civilian federal prosecution.
24. It appears that quite recently a number of civilian churchmen are becoming increasingly interested in developing a prophetic dialogue with active-duty chaplains. In late May, 1973, 14 church leaders posted letters to command chaplains at major air force installations throughout the United States and Asia. The letters urged the chaplains, as brothers in Christ, to take a stand against the continued bombing of Cambodia and to support air force personnel who refused to take part in such military activities. (See *New York Times*, "News of the Week," Section E, p. 5, Sunday, 27 May 1973. The next of the letter was reprinted in *American Report*, 4 June, 1973, p. 9.)
25. In "Some Implications of the British Experience with an All-Volunteer Army," Maurice A. Garnier states that "Writers on military matters seem to agree that military organizations will become more isolated from the rest of society" (p. 189).
26. Garnier (ibid.) finds that such has been the case in the British army.
27. Charles C. Moskos, Jr., "The Emergent Military," p. 265.
28. In 1967 virtually every officer commissioned from army ROTC was required to serve on active duty for at least a two-year period. Now the great majority of AROTC graduates spend only three months on active duty.
29. Morris Janowitz, "The Social Demography of the All-Volunteer Armed Force," p. 89.
30. Moskos, "The Emergent Military," p. 284. See also Morris Janowitz, "The Social Demography of the All-Volunteer Armed Force," p. 90 and Garnier, p. 186. Note, however, that ROTC will apparently return to Princeton University in the near future.
31. H. A. Marminion, *The Case Against a Volunteer Army*, pp. 55-56.
32. This information was obtained in private conversations with the S-5 (!) of the 197 INF BDE, Fort Benning, Georgia, 1971.
33. Marminion, p. 55.
34. Huntington, see especially Ch. 9.
35. Ibid., pp. 456-466.
36. See John S. Ambler, *Soldiers Against the State*, especially Part II, "The Army and the Nation, Isolation and Estrangement," pp. 97-153.

Further Reflections and Conclusion [151]

37. Here again I emphasize that to preserve its theological integrity, a truly prophetic chaplaincy could not "advertise" any benefits it might bring as more than by-products.

38. I now find detailed chronicles of "what's wrong with the army" more sad then shocking, and I shall not relate here what has already been widely read. Current problems in the military services are treated by the authors. Anthony B. Herbert's *Soldier* and Edward L. King's *The Death of the Army: A Pre-Mortem* supply introductions to some of the best such literature. The reference to orangutan smuggling is from G. K. Bourne, *The Ape People,* p. 342.

39. Major James S. Dickey, U.S.A., "A Personal Statement," in Russett and Stepan (eds.), p. 22. The author of *Soldier*, a retired lieutenant colonel, discusses at great length the army concept of CYA (cover your ass), according to which an officer does whatever is necessary to hide failures and preserve a perfect record, on paper, occasionally at the expense of the army (see especially p. 26).

40. Dickey, pp. 22-23.

41. Carl Thayer, unpublished paper for Yale University Department of Southeast Asia Studies, 1971.

42. From private conversations, 1973.

43. Seymour M. Hersh, *Cover-Up,* p. 128.

44. Ibid., p. 177. In recent months this chaplain has shown himself, in small, private ways, to be a person of true courage and prophetic determination.

45. God's prophets proclaim that the only missions of absolute, ultimate importance are the salvation of humanity and the establishment of Christ's kingdom. And in the final analysis, we are not responsible for these missions; God will accomplish them himself. Thus all our earthly missions are of limited importance, and their importance must be weighed against the means we would use to accomplish them.

46. A Catholic captain.

APPENDIX

MILITARY CHAPLAINS

Contents:
Cover Letter (first mailing) 156
Cover Letter (second mailing) 157
Questionnaire 158

Yale University
New Haven, Connecticut 06520

DEPARTMENT OF POLITICAL SCIENCE
5 October, 1972

Dear Chaplain:

    Four years ago, in the spring of 1968, I was serving as a rifle platoon leader with the 101st Airborne Division. At that time I became interested in the operation of the military chaplaincy: What functions does the chaplain fulfill for the Army? What services does he perform for the troops? What exactly is his proper place in a combat situation? Now, as a graduate student (and as a concerned Christian and a reserve officer) these questions still intrigue me deeply and have, in fact, become the subject of my doctoral dissertation. I have spent considerable time reading the published literature on the chaplaincy, but it presents only a partial picture. The Field Manuals are dry, lacking that human touch which only real, on-the-ground experience can provide; the popular books are poorly researched; the more formal studies are often written (I am sad to say) by academicians with obvious ideological axes to grind. I therefore learned that in order to write an honest, unbiased dissertation, I would have to approach directly those people who had first-hand contact with the Army chaplaincy.

    Naturally I should prefer to conduct my research through face-to-face interviews and personal observation, but since this is not possible I am utilizing a written survey instrument. This questionnaire, which I have enclosed, was developed after detailed study here at Yale and was further refined and improved through the careful criticism offered by more than a dozen active-duty Army chaplains. I trust that you will take the time to fill it out and return it in the stamped, self-addressed envelope which I have provided. Each questionnaire is marked with a code number which will allow me to identify those chaplains who have participated in the project. These code numbers were necessary for purposes of data-analysis, but let me assure you that no effort will be made to connect names with responses. The code numbers will be destroyed before the research project is finally prepared.

    I must advise you that this project has received no official support from the Department of Defense or the Department of the Army; it is thus a "private survey" under the terms of Paragraph 5, Section j, AR 600-46 and is therefore "neither encouraged nor discouraged" by the United States Army. I am further required by AR 600-46 to remind you that YOU MUST MAKE NO USE OF CLASSIFIED INFORMATION IN FILLING OUT THIS QUESTIONNAIRE, but of course you already knew that!

    Your help in this matter will assure a representative, balanced survey, free from the bias which might be introduced by a failure to participate. Thank you for your participation. I trust that God will care for you and will enable your ministry to prosper.

                                               Yours truly,

                                               Clarence L. Abercrombie, III

Appendix

Department of Political Science
Yale University
New Haven, Connecticut 06520
1 December, 1972

Dear Chaplain,

    Earlier this fall I sent out a letter asking your co-operation in my dissertation research on the Army chaplaincy. If you have already returned the questionnaire which I had enclosed, thank you very much; please forgive this second intrusion. There remains, however, a number of chaplains who have not replied to my first communication, perhaps because of changed addresses and problems in forwarding mail, perhaps because of lost or misplaced questionnaires, perhaps because of extended leaves or TDY. For these reasons I am sending you a second questionnaire; I really covet the participation of every chaplain in my sample. (It also occurred to me that there just **might** be some few chaplains who found it expedient to slip my questionnaire into a convenient trash can. Well, congratulations - - you too, get a second mailing, all in accordance with **Luke 18:4-5!**)

    Seriously, I do hope you will fill out and return the enclosed questionnaire. I have received many fine, painstaking responses, but if I don't have **yours**, then the survey will be incomplete and somewhat biased. Please help me to present a more nearly complete picture of the Chaplain Corps (including those chaplains who don't like questionnaires in general or my questionnaire in particular).

    Thank you so very much for your time and thoughtful effort. And oh, yes - - may you have a merry, **joyful** Christmas.

                        Yours truly,

                        Clarence L. Abercrombie, III

QUESTIONNAIRE FOR MILITARY CHAPLAINS

Code number _____

1. Place of birth: _____ 2. Date of ordination: _____
3. Briefly, why did you decide to become a clergyman? _____

_____

4. Beyond the factors stated above, are there any particular reasons for your decision to become a military chaplain? If so, please describe them briefly:

_____

Do you intend to make a career of the chaplaincy? _____

5. Did you serve a civilian parish between ordination and entry into active duty as a military chaplain? If so, please describe such service briefly:

_____

6. Did you serve in the armed forces before you became a clergyman and a chaplain? If so, please describe such service briefly:

_____

7. How many total years of civilian education (beyond high school) did you receive before entering active duty as a chaplain? _____

8. How many total months of civilian education have you received since you began your active service as a chaplain? _____

9. What academic degrees do you hold? _____

10. What service schools have you attended (*e.g.*, Chaplains Basic Course, Airborne Course, Command and General Staff College, *etc.*)?

_____

11. With what sorts of units have you spent your military ministry? (Of the unit-types listed below, please mark the one with which you have spent the greatest amount of time with a "1", the one with which you have spent the second-greatest amount of time with a "2", and so on. If you have not spent any time with a certain unit-type, simply leave it blank.)

_____ line units
_____ hospitals
_____ post chapels
_____ Army training centers
_____ service units
_____ other (Please describe:) _____

Appendix [159]

12. Of all the duty assignments you have had thus far in your military career, which was your favorite? Why? _____

_____

13. Which assignment did you like least? Why? _____

14. What is your current duty assignment? _____

15. What awards and decorations have you received? (Please include campaign medals; in the case of Bronze Star Medals and Army Commendation Medals, please indicate with a "V" if the medal was awarded for valor.) _____

How many total months have you been eligible for hostile fire pay? _____

16. How many total years have you served as a military chaplain? _____

17. To what journals and periodicals do you subscribe? _____

18. About how many hours per week do you spend studying religious and theological materials? _____

19. About how many hours per week do you spend in private prayer and devotion? _____

20. About how many times per year do you hold services for a civilian congregation? _____

21. How often do you receive communications from the civilian officials of your denomination (endorsing agency, ecclesiastical hierarchy, etc.)?

____ weekly
____ monthly
____ a couple of times a year
____ almost never

22. Do you feel that the civilian officials of your denomination show sufficient interest and concern for the needs and problems of the chaplaincy? _____

23. Of your personal friends who are also fellow clergymen,

____ virtually all are military chaplains
____ most are chaplains, but a few are civilian clergymen
____ about half are chaplains; about half are civilian clergymen
____ most are civilian clergymen, but a few are military chaplains
____ virtually all are civilian clergymen.

24. Protestant worship services in the Army have often been described as nondenominational. How do you feel about such services?

____ They present a shining example of ecumenical, Christian brotherhood that might well be copied by civilian churches.
____ They are probably helpful in building Christian unity among servicemen.

___ They are made necessary by the situation.

___ They are probably necessary but are not as desirable as separate denominations.

___ They constitute a bland, make-everybody-feel-good sort of service that precludes the presentation of serious doctrinal differences.

___ I feel that most services are not really nondenominational; rather, I think that most chaplains hold pretty much the sort of service that the civilian clergymen of their denominations hold in their separate civilian churches.

___ I am a Roman Catholic priest, so the question does not bear directly on me.
   [Note: Catholic chaplains should feel free to check any of the above options as well—if they wish.]

25. Today's military chaplain has many important tasks to fulfill. Below I have listed eleven functions which various chaplains have seen as very important. Please mark the item *you* feel is most important with a "1", the second-most important item with a "2", and so on. Please mark all items. If you feel that any item describes a function *not* appropriate for a chaplain, please mark it with an "X". Please order the functions as you would in a combat situation.

___ The chaplain helps men gain the spiritual strength that will enable them to perform their duties more effectively despite the suffering and hardships of military operations.

___ The chaplain is concerned with evangelism and conversation.

___ The chaplain helps to bolster the troops' fighting spirit and morale.

___ The chaplain counsels troops on personal problems.

___ The chaplain preaches a message of reconciliation, emphasizing that even the enemy must not be hated.

___ The chaplain helps troops make the difficult personal adjustments required by extended operations in a hostile environment.

___ The chaplain prays that God will grant victory.

___ The chaplain administers the sacraments and conducts worship services.

___ The chaplain visits with and ministers to the sick and wounded.

___ The chaplain acts as a special staff officer advising the commanding officer.

___ The chaplain stresses that obedience to the properly constituted authorities is a Christian duty.

26. While a good chaplain's work is often helpful to the Army, there *may* be occasional instances in which a chaplain feels compelled by his religious convictions to do or say something that could prove detrimental to the efficient conduct of military operations. Have such instances actually arisen in the course of your ministry?

27. What sorts of problems are most often brought to you by officers?_____

_____

by enlisted men? _____

_____

28. Do you spend more of your off-duty time with officers or enlisted men?_____

29. In what order of overall importance would *you* rate the following personnel, who might be in or attached to an infantry battalion? (Mark the most important with a "1", the second-most important with a "2", and so on. Please mark all items. To be more specific, let me suggest that the battalion is in a garrison situation but may be called into combat at very short notice; let me suggest, in fact, that the battalion under consideration is one from the 82 Airborne Division.)

___ S-1   ___ Medical Officer
___ Chaplain   ___ Maintenance Officer
___ Assistant S-3   ___ Sergeant-Major

Appendix

[161]

30. In what order of importance would the *typical enlisted man* (of the same battalion) rate the following?

___ S-1   ___ Medical Officer
___ Chaplain   ___ Maintenance Officer
___ Assistant S-3   ___ Sergeant-Major

31. In what order of importance would the *typical battalion commander* (of the same unit) rate the following?

___ S-1   ___ Medical Officer
___ Chaplain   ___ Maintenance Officer
___ Assistant S-3   ___ Sergeant-Major

* * * * * * * * * * *

32. In every chaplain's life there must obviously be times of action and times of contemplation, and he cannot affirm either quality to the *total* exclusion of the other. Yet most men probably lean in one direction or the other — and some very definitely so. On the following scale, please circle the number which you feel would best describe your own orientation:

CONTEMPLATIVE   MAN OF ACTION

1   2   3   4   5

33. Overall, do you feel yourself more nearly oriented toward the values of nationalism or to those of a united world?

NATIONALISM   WORLD UNION

1   2   3   4   5

34. Do you tend to agree or disagree with the following statement? "In international relations, the interests of the United States should always come first."

AGREE   DISAGREE

1   2   3   4   5

35. Do you agree or disagree with the following statement? "An insult to your honor should not be forgotten."

AGREE   DISAGREE

1   2   3   4   5

36. Do you think that you should remain very sensitive to human suffering, or do you feel you have to steel yourself to some extent so that you will be better able to carry out your duties in the face of such suffering?

REMAIN VERY SENSITIVE   STEEL MYSELF SOMEWHAT

1   2   3   4   5

37. Do you feel it would be morally right to bomb (with nuclear weapons) the civilian population centers of an enemy nation in retaliation for similar attacks on our own population centers?

MORALLY RIGHT   MORALLY WRONG
TO BOMB   TO BOMB

1   2   3   4   5
....

38. For the "average person" (assuming for the moment there is such a thing), is war more likely to bring out the best or the worst qualities?

BEST QUALITIES   WORST QUALITIES

1   2   3   4   5
....

39. It probably requires a very special sort of person to fulfill effectively the challenging vocation of the military chaplaincy. Below I have listed fourteen descriptive phrases. Some of them are appropriate for describing a military chaplain; others are inappropriate. Some may be neutral. In the spaces provided, please mark with a "1" the quality you feel is most important for a chaplain to possess. Mark the second-most important with a "2", and so on. Please mark all items.

___ boastful
___ strict
___ willing to forgive an offender again and again
___ willing to use violence to obtain justice
___ kind
___ feels killing in war is justified
___ believes in God as the final authority and absolute ruler over all men and nations
___ aggressive
___ meticulously avoids all "foul" or "improper" language
___ quick-tempered
___ unconditional in loyalty to the United States
___ loves enemies
___ gentle
___ dislikes involvement in any form of violence

Using the numbers with which you rated the above items, please tell which qualities you feel would be a positive help to the chaplain, which you feel would be neutral, and which you feel would be detrimental:

I believe that the qualities I marked with numbers *1* through ___ would be helpful; those I marked with numbers ___ through ___ would be neutral; those I marked with numbers ___ through *14* would be detrimental.

40. Assume that you are serving as chaplain to a combat infantry unit. One day, after the unit has returned to a relatively secure base camp, a soldier comes to you and says that he believes God does not wish for him to participate further in the war. The soldier expresses his desire to become a conscientious objector. Briefly, what do you do?

_____

_____

_____

What do you think the unit commander would want you to do? _____

_____

* * * * * * * * *

[The following questions on participation in war lie at the heart of my study. The responses which I have indicated for each questions are, of course, gross over-simplifications of much broader theological, political, or ethical positions. In choosing which answers you think are appropriate, I trust you will think not so much of my caricatured condensations as of the overall positions — with which you are probably more familiar than I.]

Appendix [163]

41. Theologicans, ethicists, and political scientists have long argued over the conditions under which it is right for a person to participate in a war. Please check the answer below which you feel best describes the conditions under which a Christian may participate in a war:

____ A Christian is permitted to participate in any war legally declared by the legitimate political authorities constituted over him. (Position 1)

____ A Christian is permitted to participate in any war that seeks only to further some great cause ordained by God. (Position 2)

____ A Christian is permitted to participate in a war when: a) the war is fought for a cause that is basically just; b) the evil that would occur as a result of not fighting the war would be greater than the evil inherent in the combat itself; c) the war is fought in the most humane possible manner with certain rules of war observed no matter what. (Position 3)

____ There are no conditions under which it is ethically permissible for a Christian to participate in war.

____ A Christian may participate in war only when some combination of the above conditions exists (Which Positions? _____)

____ It is senseless to talk about conditions for Christian participation in war; men do not choose to participate in war but are dragged into war by forces beyond their control.

42. Suppose you were asked to serve as a chaplain in a war which you felt Christians should not be made to fight. What would you do?

____ I would not serve, and I would urge others to refuse to serve – as soldiers or chaplains.

____ I would not serve, but I would not urge others to refuse to serve; each person must make up his own mind.

____ I would find the question of participation very difficult, and I really don't know exactly what I'd do.

____ My vocation is not to judge the sort of war the Army may have to fight but is rather to minister unto those men who find themselves fighting it.

43. Besides the debate over the general matter of Christian participation in war, there has also been serious questioning over what sorts of actions are permissible in a combat situation. Please check the item below which best describes your views on what actions a Christian is and is not permitted to take in wartime:

____ A Christian is permitted to carry out any orders given by the officers and non-commissioned officers who have been lawfully appointed as his superiors.

____ A Christian is permitted to take any action that will contribute to the chances of winning victory and shortening war.

____ A Christian is not permitted to commit certain actions that are generally well-known and are prohibited by international laws of civilized warfare (for example, the intentional killing of well-marked medical personnel).

44. In almost every war there have been reports of soldiers being ordered to kill enemy prisoners. Had a chaplain been present when such orders were given, what should he have done?

_____

_____

_____

45. Let us now consider an imaginary situation. An infantry battalion has been pulled out of the battle line for six weeks of rest and recuperation. At the end of this period, the battalion will again go back into combat. The battalion commander is sincerely worried about morale; the usual remedies of movies, ice cream, mail, and training have not worked, and the CO fears he will have to go back into the field with dispirited men. He therefore

decides to set up (unofficially, of course) a temporary brothel for purposes of raising morale. The chaplain attached to the battalion gets wind of the idea. He talks with the battalion commander, attempting to explain that there will be no real, lasting gains in morale. Nevertheless, the CO is convinced that his idea will work. What should the chaplain do?

46. Despite the recently publicized lapses, it would seem that the record of the US Army concerning war atrocities is really quite excellent. What do you feel is the role of the chaplain in preventing atrocities?

____ The chaplain really has no special role at all. Any well-trained, professionally competent American officer (whatever his religious commitment) will take whatever steps are necessary to insure that atrocities are not committed.

____ The chaplain has a very important role in assuring that the members of an Army command are kept at a level of moral fitness so that they will not commit atrocities. In some ways, the chaplain acts as a conscience to the Army.

____ I have another way of looking at this issue. (Please explain: _____

_____)

47. Some of the military chaplaincy's more radical critics contend that the chaplaincy serves chiefly a legitimating function, that the presence in the Army of priests and ministers helps convince would-be pacifistic Christians that God really does approve of participation in military service and war. How would you answer such criticisms? (Note: If you tend to have a natural, violent reaction to this sort of criticism, please attempt to refrain from ripping up this questionnaire and tossing it into the trash can. You are so near the end!)____

Do you ever feel a serious conflict of values because of the dual nature of your clergyman-officer role?_____

48. Here is one last question before I let you get back to work. This one presents another imaginary situation — in fact, it is (to use a youth culture expression) "far out." Nevertheless, I do hope you'll answer it, for I'd really like to use it in my analysis. Many chaplains feel that they minister to soldiers as people, without taking into consideration the political justice of the cause for which they may be fighting. Suppose you found out that there were, in the army of another nation, a number of Christians who badly needed the service of a minister or priest (who could not be found among the citizens of their own country). If you were not in the US Army, would you feel you could serve those men as a chaplain

____ with the British Army?

____ with the Swedish Army?

____ with the Soviet Army?

____ with the North Vietnamese Army?

____ I could morally serve as a chaplain to no army besides that of the United States.

Throughout much of this questionnaire I have asked you to answer some very complex questions in a very limited space. Such a "fixed choice" format is necessary for the type of data-analysis I wish to use. Nevertheless, I know (from personal experience in answering questionnaires) that it can be frustrating to have well thought-out opinions compressed into a word or two. So, if you wish (and if you have the time) I hope you will use all the space necessary to make any comments you would like about questions I have included, about the chaplaincy, about the Army, about the problem of Christian participation in war, about Christianity itself.

Appendix

I want to thank you most sincerely for your participation in this project. As I said in my cover letter, I think there is something important that can be learned from a study of Army chaplains — something with a value that goes beyond my short-range goal of passing my dissertation. (If I didn't think so, I would have picked an easier topic!) Thank you again — and God bless you.

CIVILIAN CLERGYMEN

Contents:
Cover Letter (first mailing) 168
Cover Letter (second mailing) 169
Questionnnaire 170

Yale University
New Haven, Connecticut 06520

DEPARTMENT OF POLITICAL SCIENCE

October 5, 1972

Dear Sir:

    I am presently at Yale University's Department of Political Science, engaged in research on the inter-relationship of Church and State. My doctoral dissertation will focus primarily on the attitudes of Army chaplains; however, in order to analyze such attitudes from the proper perspective, it will be vitally important for me to know a good deal about the views of civilian clergymen. Naturally I should prefer to conduct my research through face-to-face interviews, but since that is not possible I am utilizing a written survey instrument. This questionnaire, which I have enclosed, was developed after detailed study here at Yale and was further refined and improved through the careful criticism offered by more than two dozen priests and ministers. I trust that you will take the time to fill it out and return it in the stamped, self-addressed envelope which I have provided.

    Your help in this matter will assure a representative, unbiased survey, free from the problems which would be introduced by a failure to participate. Thank you for your consideration. I trust that God will care for you and will enable your ministry to prosper.

Yours truly,

Clarence L. Abercrombie, III

Clarence L. Abercrombie, III

Appendix

Department of Political Science
Yale University
New Haven, Connecticut 06520
1 December, 1972

Dear Sir,

    Earlier this fall I sent out a letter asking your co-operation in my dissertation research on the Army chaplaincy. I needed to know the views of civilian clergymen on several different subjects in order to compare them with those of chaplains. If you have already returned the questionnaire which I had enclosed, thank you very much; please forgive this second intrusion. There remains, however, a number of clergymen who have not replied to my first communication, perhaps because of changed addresses and problems in forwarding mail, perhaps because of lost or misplaced questionnaires. For these reasons I am sending you a second questionnaire; I really covet the participation of **every** clergyman in my sample. (It also occurred to me that there **might** be some few clergymen who found it expedient to slip my questionnaire into a convenient trash can. Well, congratulations - - you too, get a second mailing, all in accordance with **Luke 18: 4-5!**)

    Seriously, I do hope you will fill out and return the enclosed questionnaire. I have received many fine, painstaking responses, but if I don't have **yours**, then the survey will be incomplete and somewhat biased. Please help me to present a more nearly complete picture of your denomination (including those clergymen who don't like questionnaires in general or my questionnaire in particular).

    Thank you so very much for your time and thoughtful effort. And oh, yes - - may you have a merry, **joyful** Christmas.

Yours truly,

Clarence L. Abercrombie, III

Clarence L. Abercrombie, III

QUESTIONNAIRE FOR CIVILIAN CLERGYMEN

1. Date of birth: _____ 2. Denomination: _____
3. Place of birth: _____ 4. Date of ordination: _____

5. Briefly, why did you decide to become a clergyman? _____
_____

6. Do you intend to make the ministry/priesthood your life's work? _____
7. Have you ever served in the armed forces? ____ If so, did you serve as a chaplain? ____
8. How many total years of education (beyond high school) have you received? ____
9. What academic degrees do you hold? _____
_____

10. What is the nature of your current vocational duties? _____
_____

11. For how many years have you been a clergyman? _____
_____

12. About how many hours per week do you spend studying religious and theological materials? _____

13. About how many hours per week do you spend in private prayer and devotion? ____

14. Today's chaplain is called upon to perform a specialized ministry which includes many important tasks. Below I have listed eleven functions which various chaplains have seen as very important. Please mark the item *you* feel is most important with a "1", the second-most important item with a "2", and so on. Please mark all items. If you feel that any item describes a function *not* appropriate for a chaplain, please mark it with an "X". Please order the functions as you would in a combat situation.

____ The chaplain helps men gain the spiritual strength that will enable them to perform their duties more effectively despite the suffering and hardships of military operations.
____ The chaplain is concerned with evangelism and conversion.
____ The chaplain helps to bolster the troops' fighting spirit and morale.
____ The chaplain counsels troops on personal problems.
____ The chaplain preaches a message of reconciliation, emphasizing that even the enemy must not be hated.
____ The chaplain helps troops make the difficult personal adjustments required by extended operations in a hostile environment.
____ The chaplain prays that God will grant victory.
____ The chaplain administers the sacraments and conducts worship services.
____ The chaplain visits with and ministers to the sick and wounded.
____ The chaplain acts as a special staff officer advising the commanding officer.
____ The chaplain stresses that obedience to the properly constituted authorities is a Christian duty.

Appendix [171]

15. While a good chaplain's work is often helpful to the Army, there *may* be occasional instances in which a chaplain feels compelled by his religious convictions to do or say something that could prove detrimental to the efficient conduct of military operations. Would you think that the average chaplain, at some time in his career, has been faced with such a situation?

16. In every clergyman's life there must obviously be times of action and times of contemplation, and he cannot affirm either quality to the *total* exclusion of the other. Yet most men probably lean in one direction or the other—and some very definitely so. On the following scale, please circle the number which you feel would best describe your own orientation:

CONTEMPLATIVE   MAN OF ACTION

1   2   3   4   5
....

17. Overall, do you feel yourself more nearly oriented toward the values of nationalism or to those of a united world?

NATIONALISM   WORLD UNION

1   2   3   4   5
....

18. Do you tend to agree or disagree with the following statement? "In international relations, the interests of the United States should always come first."

AGREE   DISAGREE

1   2   3   4   5
....

19. Do you agree or disagree with the following statement? "An insult to your honor should not be forgotten."

AGREE   DISAGREE

1   2   3   4   5
....

20. Do you think you should remain very sensitive to human suffering, or do you feel you have to steel yourself to some extent so that you will be better able to carry out your duties in the face of such suffering?

REMAIN VERY   STEEL MYSELF
SENSITIVE   SOMEWHAT

1   2   3   4   5
....

21. Do you feel it would be morally right to bomb (with nuclear weapons) the civilian population centers of an enemy nation in retaliation for similar attacks on our own population centers?

MORALLY RIGHT   MORALLY WRONG
TO BOMB   TO BOMB

1   2   3   4   5
....

[172]

22. For the "average person" (assuming for the moment there is such a thing), is war more likely to bring out the best or the worst qualities?

BEST QUALITIES				WORST QUALITIES
1	2	3	4	5

....

23. It probably requires a very special sort of person to fulfill effectively the challenges of the clergyman's vocation. Below I have listed fourteen descriptive phrases. Some of them are appropriate for describing a clergyman; others are inappropriate. Some may be neutral. In the spaces provided, please mark with a "1" the quality you feel is most important for a clergyman to possess. Mark the second-most important with a "2", and so on. Please mark all items.

___ boastful
___ strict
___ willing to forgive an offender again and again
___ willing to use violence to obtain justice
___ kind
___ feels killing in war is justified
___ believes in God as the final authority and absolute ruler over all men and nations
___ aggressive
___ meticulously avoids all "foul" or "improper" language
___ quick-tempered
___ unconditional in loyalty to the United States
___ loves enemies
___ gentle
___ dislikes involvement in any form of violence

Using the numbers with which you rated the above items, please tell which qualities you feel would be a positive help to the clergyman, which you feel would be neutral, and which you feel would be detrimental:

___ I believe that the qualities I marked with numbers 1 through __ would be helpful; those I marked with numbers __ through __ would be neutral; those I marked with numbers __ through 14 would be detrimental.

[The following questions on participation in war lie at the heart of my study. The responses which I have indicated for each question are, of course, gross over-simplifications of much broader theological, political, or ethical positions. In choosing which answers you think are appropriate, I trust you will think not so much of my caricatured condensations as of the overall positions—with which you are probably more familiar than I.]

23. Theologians, ethicists, and political scientists have long argued over the conditions under which it is right for a person to participate in a war. Please check the answer below which you feel best describes the conditions under which a Christian may participate in a war:

___ A Christian is permitted to participate in any way legally declared by the legitimate political authorities constituted over him. (Position 1)

___ A Christian is permitted to participate in any war that seeks only to further some great cause ordained by God. (Position 2)

___ A Christian is permitted to participate in a war when: a) the war is fought for a cause that is basically just; b) the evil that would occur as a result of not fighting the war would be greater than the evil inherent in the combat itself; c) the war is fought in the most humane possible manner with certain rules of war observed no matter what. (Position 3)

___ There are no conditions under which it is ethically permissible for a Christian to participate in war.

___ A Christian may participate in war only when some combination of the above conditions exist. (Which Positions?_____)

___ It is senseless to talk about conditions for Christian participation in war; men do not choose to participate in war but are dragged into war by forces beyond their control.

Appendix [173]

24. Besides the debate over the general matter of Christian participation in war, there has also been serious questioning over what sorts of actions are permissible in a combat situation. Please check the item below which best describes your views on what actions a Christian is and is not permitted to take in wartime:

___ A Christian is permitted to carry out any orders given by the officers and non-commissioned officers who have been lawfully appointed as his superiors.

___ A Christian is permitted to take any action that will contribute to the chances of winning victory and shortening the war.

___ A Christian is not permitted to commit certain actions that are generally well-known and are prohibited by international laws of civilized warfare (for the example, the intentional killing of well-marked medical personnel).

25. Imagine this situation, which could confront the chaplain of a combat infantry unit. One day, after the unit has returned to a relatively secure base camp, a soldier goes to the chaplain and says that he believes God does not wish for him to participate further in the war. The soldier expresses his desire to become a conscientious objector. What do you believe the average chaplain *will* do?

_____

_____

_____

What do you feel the chaplain *should* do? _____

_____

_____

26. Despite the recently publicized lapses, it would seem that the record of the US Army concerning war atrocities is really quite excellent. What do you feel is the role of the chaplain in preventing atrocities?

___ The chaplain really has no special role at all. Any well-trained, professionally competent American officer (whatever his religious commitment) will take whatever steps are necessary to insure that atrocities are not committed.

___ The chaplain has a very important role in assuring that the members of an Army command are kept at a level of moral fitness so that they will not commit atrocities. In some ways, the chaplain acts as a conscience to the Army.

I have another way of looking at this issue. (Please explain: _____

_____

_____

MILITARY OFFICERS

Contents:
Cover Letter (first mailing) 176
Cover Letter (second mailing) 177
Questionnaire 178

Yale University New Haven, Connecticut 06520

DEPARTMENT OF POLITICAL SCIENCE
4 October, 1972

Dear Sir:

Four years ago, in the spring of 1968, I was serving in Viet-Nam as a rifle platoon leader with the 101st Airborne Division. At that time I became interested in the operation of the military chaplaincy: What functions does the chaplain fulfill for the Army? What services does he perform for the troops? What exactly is his proper place in a combat situation? Now, as a graduate student (and as a reserve officer) these questions still intrigue me deeply and have, in fact, become the subject of my doctoral dissertation. I have spent considerable time reading the published literature on the chaplaincy, but it presents only a partial picture. The Field Manuals are dry, lacking the human touch that only real, on-the-ground experience can provide; the popular books are poorly researched; the more formal studies are often written (I am sad to say) by academicians with obvious ideological axes to grind. I therefore learned that in order to write an honest, unbiased dissertation, I would have to approach directly those people who have had first-hand contacts with Army chaplains.

A good deal of my research will deal with the chaplains themselves, but another part, equally important, will involve a select group of military officers (such as yourself) who have significant administrative/supervisory contact with members of the Chaplains Corps. Naturally I should prefer to conduct my research through face-to-face interviews and personal observation, but since this is not possible I am utilizing a written survey instrument. This questionnaire, which I have enclosed, was developed after detailed study here at Yale and was further refined and improved through the careful criticism offered by more than a dozen active-duty Army officers. I trust that you will take the time to fill it out and return it in the stamped, self-addressed envelope which I have provided.

I must advise you that this project has received no official support from the Department of Defense or the Department of the Army; it is thus a "private survey" under the terms of Paragraph 5, Section j, AR 600-46 and is therefore "neither encouraged nor discouraged" by the United States Army. I am further required by AR 600-46 to remind you that YOU MUST MAKE NO USE OF CLASSIFIED INFORMATION IN FILLING OUT THIS QUESTIONNAIRE, but of course you already knew that!

Your help in this matter will assure a representative, balanced survey, free from the bias which might be introduced by a failure to participate. Thank you.

Yours truly,

Clarence L. Abercrombie, III

Clarence L. Abercrombie, III

Appendix

Department of Political Science
Yale University
New Haven, Connecticut 06520
1 December, 1972

Dear Sir:

    Earlier this fall I sent out a letter asking your co-operation in my dissertation research on the Army chaplaincy. I needed to know the views of military commanders on sereral different subjects in order to compare them with those of chaplains. If you have already returned the questionnaire which I had enclosed, thank you very much; please forgive this second intrusion. There remains, however, a number of military officers who have not replied to my first communication. To you I am sending a second questionnaire, for I really covet the participation of every unit or installation commander in my sample.

    I do hope you will fill out and return the enclosed questionnaire. I have received many fine, painstaking responses, but if I don't have **yours**, then the survey will be incomplete and somewhat biased. Please help me to present a more nearly complete picture of the Army's commanding officers. (I already have a nice set of responses from officers who **liked** my questionnaire, but I remember enough from my Army days to know many of you don't like it all that much. And you are the very men whose opinions I most need if I am to present a fair picture of the Army.) Thank you very much for your time and thoughtful effort. I hope that you will have a happy holiday season.

                            Yours truly,

                            Clarence L. Abercrombie, III

QUESTIONNAIRE FOR MILITARY OFFICERS

1. Rank and branch: _____ 2. Date of birth: _____
3. Component (USAR, RA, etc.): _____
4. Religious affiliation: _____ 5. Place of birth: _____
6. Do you intend to make a career of military service? _____
7. How many total years of civilian education (beyond high school) did you receive before entering active duty? _____
8. How many total months of civilian education have you received since you entered active duty? _____
9. What academic degrees do you hold? _____
10. What service schools have you attended (e.g., Branch Basic Course, Airborne Course, Command and General Staff College, etc.)? _____

11. What is your current duty assignment? _____
12. What awards and decorations have you received? (Please include campaign medals; in the case of Bronze Star Medals and Army Commendation Medals, please indicate with a "V" if the medal was awarded for valor.) _____

How many total months have you been eligible for hostile fire pay? _____
13. How many total years have you served in the armed forces? _____
How many of those years have you served as a commissioned officer? _____

[The next four questions will be directly concerned with military chaplains.]

14. Today's military chaplain has many important tasks to fulfill. Below I have listed eleven functions which various chaplains have seen as very important. Please mark the item *you* feel is most important with a "1", the second-most important item with a "2", and so on. Please mark all items. If you feel that any item describes a function *not* appropriate for a chaplain, please mark it with an "X". Please order the functions as you would in a combat situation.

___ The chaplain helps men gain the spiritual strength that will enable them to perform their duties more effectively despite the suffering and hardships of military operations.
___ The chaplain is concerned with evangelism and conversion.
___ The chaplain helps to bolster the troops' fighting spirit and morale.
___ The chaplain counsels troops on personal problems.
___ The chaplain preaches a message of reconciliation, emphasizing that even the enemy must not be hated.
___ The chaplain helps troops make the difficult personal adjustments required by extended operations in a hostile environment.
___ The chaplain prays that God will grant victory.
___ The chaplain administers the sacraments and conducts worship services.
___ The chaplain visits with and ministers to the sick and wounded.
___ The chaplain acts as a special staff officer advising the commanding officer.
___ The chaplain stresses that obedience to the properly constituted authorities is a Christian duty.

Appendix [179]

15. While a good chaplain's work is often helpful to the Army, there *may* be occasional instances in which a chaplain feels compelled by his religious convictions to do or say something that could prove detrimental to the efficient conduct of military operations. Are you aware of any such instances that have actually occurred?_____

16. Do you believe the work of the chaplain should be directed more towards officers or enlisted men?_____ Why?_____

17. If you were the commanding officer of an infantry battalion, in what order of importance would you rate the following personnel, who might be in or attached to your unit? (Mark the most important with a "1", the second-most important with a "2", and so on. To be more specific, let me suggest that the battalion is in a garrison situation but may be called into combat at very short notice; let me suggest, in fact, that the battalion under consideration is one from the 82 Airborne Division.)

___ S-1 ___ Medical Officer
___ Chaplain ___ Maintenance Officer
___ Assistant S-3 ___ Sergeant-Major

18. In every military officer's life there must obviously be times of action and times of contemplation, and he cannot affirm either quality to the *total* exclusion of the other. Yet most men lean in one direction or the other—and some very definitely so. On the following scale, please circle the number which you feel would best describe your own orientation:

CONTEMPLATIVE   MAN OF ACTION
1   2   3   4   5

19. Overall, do you feel yourself more nearly oriented toward the values of nationalism or toward those of a united world?

NATIONALISM   UNITED WORLD
1   2   3   4   5

20. Do you tend to agree or disagree with the following statement? "In international relations, the interests of the United States should always come first."

AGREE   DISAGREE
1   2   3   4   5

21. Do you agree or disagree with the following statement? "An insult to your honor should not be forgotten."

AGREE   DISAGREE
1   2   3   4   5

22. Do you think that you should remain very sensitive to human suffering, or do you feel you have to steel yourself to some extent so that you will be better able to carry out your duties in the face of such suffering?

REMAIN VERY   STEEL MYSELF
SENSITIVE   SOMEWHAT
1   2   3   4   5

23. Do you feel it would be morally right to bomb (with nuclear weapons) the civilian population centers of an enemy nation in retaliation for similar attacks on our own population centers?

MORALLY RIGHT TO BOMB				MORALLY WRONG TO BOMB
1	2	3	4	5

24. For the "average person" (assuming for the moment there is such a thing), is war more likely to bring out the best or the worst qualities?

BEST QUALITIES				WORST QUALITIES
1	2	3	4	5

25. It probably requires a very special sort of person to fulfill effectively the challenges of the military profession. Below I have listed fourteen descriptive phrases. Some of them are appropriate for describing a professional military officer; others are inappropriate. Some may be neutral. In the spaces provided, please mark with a "1" the quality you feel is most important for a military officer to possess. Mark the second-most important with a "2", and so on. Please mark all items.

___ boastful
___ strict
___ willing to forgive an offender again and again
___ willing to use violence to obtain justice
___ kind
___ feels killing in war is justified
___ believes in God as the final authority and absolute ruler over all men and nations
___ aggressive
___ meticulously avoids all "foul" or "improper" language
___ quick-tempered
___ unconditional in loyalty to the United States
___ loves enemies
___ gentle
___ dislikes involvement in any form of violence

Using the numbers with which you rated the above items, please tell which qualities you feel would be a positive help to the military officer, which you feel would be neutral, and which you feel would be detrimental:

___ I believe that the qualities I marked with numbers 1 through ___ would be helpful; those I marked with numbers ___ through ___ would be neutral; those I marked with numbers ___ through 14 would be detrimental.

26. Assume that you are the commanding officer of a combat infantry unit. One day, after the unit has returned to a relatively secure base camp, a soldier goes to the chaplain and says that he believes God does not wish for him to participate further in the war. The solider expresses his desire to become a conscientious objector. What do you believe the average chaplain *will* do?

_____

_____

What do you feel the chaplain *should* do? _____

_____

27. Despite the recently publicized lapses, it would seem that the record of the US Army concerning war atrocities is really quite excellent. What do you feel is the role of the chaplain in preventing atrocities?

Appendix [181]

___ The chaplain really has no special role at all. Any well-trained, professionally competent American officer (whatever his religious commitment) will take whatever steps are necessary to insure that atrocities are not committed.

___ The chaplain has a very important role in assuring that the members of an Army command are kept at a level of moral fitness so that they will not commit atrocities. In some ways, the chaplain acts as a conscience to the Army.

___ I have another way of looking at this issue. (Please explain: _____

BIBLIOGRAPHY

Abelson, Robert P., et al. *Theories of Cognitive Consistency: A Sourcebook.* Skokie, Ill.: Rand McNally, 1968.
Abercrombie, Clarence L., III. "Bases in Modern Protestant Theology for a Doctrine of Resistance to the Unjust State: Barth and Bonhoeffer." *Religion in Life,* Autumn 1973, pp. 344-359.
– – –. "Politicization: The Military and Other American Professions." New Haven, Conn.: Unpublished general examination paper for Yale University's Department of Political Science, 1971.
Ahlstrom, Sydney E. "The American National Faith: Humane, Yet All Too Human." In *Religion and the Humanizing of Man: Plenary Addresses, International Congress of Learned Societies in the Field of Religion.* James M. Robinson, Ed. Los Angeles: Council on the Study of Religion, 1972, pp. 101-129.
– – –. "The National Faith: Where Did It Go? How Can We Find It in 1973?" *Yale Alumni Magazine.* January 1973, pp. 8-9.
– – –. *A Religious History of the American People.* New Haven, Conn.: Yale University Press, 1972.
Ambler, John S. *Soldiers Against the State: The French Army in Politics.* Garden City, N.Y.: Doubleday.
Appelquist, A. Ray, Ed. *Church, State and Chaplaincy: Essays and Statements on the American Chaplaincy System.* Washington, D.C.: General Commission on Chaplains and Armed Forces Personnel, 1969.
Aquinas, Thomas. *Summa Theologicae* (1256-1272), Part II. Chicago: Encyclopaedia Britannica, 1953.
Aronis, Alexander B. *A Comparative Study of the Opinions of Navy Chaplains and their Commanding Officers on the Role Expectations, Deficiencies, and Preferred In-Service Education for Navy Chaplains.* Washington, D.C.: Unpublished Ph.D. thesis, American University, 1971.
Augustine. *Concerning the City of God Against the Pagans* (written 413-426, first published 1467). Translated by Henry Bettenson. Middlesex: Pelican, 1972.
Avineri, Shlomo. *The Social and Political Thought of Karl Marx.* Cambridge: Cambridge University Press, 1969.
Bainton, Roland. *Christian Attitudes Toward War and Peace: A Historical Survey and Critical Re-evaluation.* Nashville, Tenn.: Abingdon Press, 1960.
Bakunin, Michael. *God and the State* (1882). New York: Dover, 1970.

Barth, Karl. *Church Dogmatics,* Vol. III/4, *The Doctrine of Creation,* G. W. Bromiley and T. F. Torrance, Eds., translated by A. T. MacKay et al. Edinburgh: T. & T. Clark, 1961.
Bentz, W. Kenneth. "Consensus Between Role Expectations and Role Behavior Among Ministers." *Community Mental Health.* Vol. IV, No. 4, 1968, pp. 301-306.
Berger, Peter L. *The Precarious Vision: A Sociologist Looks at Social Fictions and the Christian Faith.* Garden City, N.Y.: Doubleday, 1961.
―――. *The Sacred Canopy: Elements of a Sociological Theory of Religion.* Garden City, N.Y.: Anchor Books, 1969.
Bonhoeffer, Dietrich. *Letters and Papers from Prison* (1951). E. Bethge, Ed., translated by R. Fuller. New York: Macmillan, 1953.
Bourne, G. H. *The Ape People.* New York: Putnam, 1971.
Burchard, Waldo W. "Role Conflicts of Military Chaplains." *American Sociological Review,* October 1954, pp. 528-535.
―――. *The Role of the Military Chaplain.* Unpublished Ph.D. thesis, University of California, Berkeley, 1953.
Bushman, Richard L. *From Puritan to Yankee: Character and the Social Order in Connecticut, 1690-1775.* New York: Norton, 1967.
Cherry, Conrad, Ed. *God's New Israel: Religious Interpretations of American Destiny.* Englewood Cliffs, N.J.: Prentice-Hall, 1971.
Clergy and Laity Concerned. This group collectively sent a letter to air force chaplains; the letter was reproduced in *American Report,* 4 June, 1973, p. 9.
Cox, Harvey G., Ed. *Military Chaplains: From a Religious Military to a Military Religion.* New York: American Report Press, 1971.
Davis, David Brion, Ed. *Ante-Bellum Reform.* New York: Harper & Row, 1967.
Deagle, Dewin A., Jr. "Contemporary Professionalism and Future Military Leadership." *Annals of the American Academy of Political and Social Sciences: The Military and American Society,* March 1973, pp. 162-170.
Durkheim, Emil. *Suicide: A Study in Sociology* (1897). Edited by and with an introduction by George Simpson, translated by John Spaulding and George Simpson. New York: Free Press, 1951.
Easton, David. *A Systems Analysis of Political Life.* New York: Wiley, 1965.
Einaudi, Luigi, et al. *Latin American Institutional Development: The Changing Catholic Church.* Santa Monica, Calif.: RAND Corporation, 1969.
―――. "Onward Christian Soldiers." *Latin America,* 25 May 1973, pp. 166-167.
Feuerbach, Ludwig Andreas. *The Essence of Christianity.* Introduction by Karl Barth, translated by George Eliot. New York: Harper & Row, 1957.
Filler, Louis. *The Crusade Against Slavery, 1830-1860.* New York: Harper & Row, 1960.
Finn, James. *Conscience and Command: Justice and Discipline in the Military.* New York: Random House, 1971.
Finney, D. J. *Probit Analysis: A Statistical Treatment of the Sigmoid Curve.* Cambridge: Cambridge University Press, 1947.
Fontaine, André. *History of the Cold War.* (See especially Vol. I, *From the October Revolution to the Korean War, 1917-1950.*) Translated by D. D. Paige. New York: Random House, 1970.
Garnier, Maurice A. "Some Implications of the British Experience with an All-Volunteer Army." *Pacific Sociological Review,* April 1973, pp. 177-191.

Bibliography [185]

Goffman, Erving. *The Presentation of Self in Everyday Life.* Garden City, N.Y.: Doubleday, 1959.
Goldberger, Arthur S. *Econometric Theory.* New York: Wiley, 1964.
Hely, Joe. "Command Influence on Military Justice." *St. Louis University Law Journal,* Winter 1970, pp. 300-310.
Herbert, Anthony B. (Lt. Col., Ret.), with James T. Wooten. *Soldier.* New York: Holt, Rinehart & Winston, 1973.
Hersh, Seymour M. *Cover-Up: The Army's Secret Investigation of the Massacre at My Lai 4.* New York: Random House, 1972.
Hobbes, Thomas. *Leviathan* (1651). Harmondsworth, England: Penguin Books, 1968.
Homans, George C. *The Human Group.* New York: Harcourt Brace Jovanovich, 1950.
Honeywell, Roy J. (Chaplain, Col., U.S.A., Ret.). *Chaplains of the United States Army.* Washington, D.C.: Office of the Chief of Chaplains, Department of the Army, 1958.
Hope, Christine A. "Town Development and Social Change in Colonial Connecticut." New Haven, Conn.: Unpublished paper for Yale University's Department of Sociology, 1971.
Hudson, Winthrop S. Ed. *Nationalism and Religion in America: Concepts of American Identity and Mission.* New York: Harper & Row, 1970.
Huntington, Samuel P. *The Soldier and the State: The Theory and Politics of Civil-Military Relations.* New York: Vintage Books, 1957.
Janowitz, Morris. *The Professional Soldier: A Social and Political Portrait.* New York: Free Press, 1971 ed.
----. "The Social Demography of the All-Volunteer Armed Force." *Annals of the American Academy of Political and Social Science: The Military and American Society,* March 1973, pp. 86-93.
Johnston, J. *Econometric Methods.* New York: McGraw-Hill, 1963.
Kahn, Robert L., et al. *Organizational Stress: Studies in Role Conflict and Ambiguity.* New York: Wiley, 1964.
Keys, Clifford E., Jr. *Student Research Project 86: An Evaluation of Certain Factors Affecting the Retention Rate of Career Chaplains in the United States Army.* Unpublished master's thesis for the Industrial College of the Armed Forces, Washington, D.C., 1969.
Kiesler, Charles A., et al. *Attitude Change: A Critical Analysis of Theoretical Approaches.* New York: Wiley, 1969.
King, Edward L. *The Death of the Army: A Pre-Mortem.* New York: Saturday Review Press, 1972.
Laymon, Charles M., Ed. *The Interpreter's One-Volume Commentary on the Bible.* Nashville, Tenn.: Abingdon Press, 1971.
Licklider, Roy E. *The Private Nuclear Strategists.* Columbus: Ohio State University Press, 1971.
The Lincoln Library of Essential Information. Buffalo, N.Y.: Frontier Press Company, 1961.
Locke, John. *The Second Treatise on Government* (1689). New York: Liberal Arts Press, 1952.
Luther, Martin. "Temporal Authority: To What Extent it Should Be Obeyed" (1523), in *Selected Writings of Martin Luther,* Vol. II. Edited by Theodore G. Tappert. Philadelphia: Fortress Press, 1967.

———. *Whether Soldiers, too, Can Be Saved* (1527), in *Selected Writings of Martin Luther*, Vol. III.
Lutheran Church in America. *1972 Yearbook, Lutheran Church in America.* Philadelphia: Board of Publication of the Lutheran Church in America, 1972.
MacFarlane, Norman. "Navy Chaplaincy: Muzzled Ministry." *The Christian Century*, 2 November 1966, pp. 1338-1339.
Machiavelli, Niccolo. *The Prince and the Discourses* (1513 and 1519, respectively). New York: Modern Library, 1950.
MacKenzie, Kenneth M. *The Robe and the Sword: The Methodist Church and the Rise of American Imperialism.* Washington, D.C.: Public Affairs Press, 1961.
Marmion, Harry A. *The Case Against a Volunteer Army.* New York: Quadrangle, 1971.
Marx, Karl, and Friedrich Engels. *On Religion* (1841-1895). Introduction by Reinhold Niebuhr. New York: Schocken Books, 1967; reprinted from 1957 edition published by the Foreign Languages Publishing House, Moscow.
Mathews, Donald G. *Slavery and Methodism: A Chapter in American Morality, 1780-1845.* Princeton, N.J.: Princeton University Press, 1965.
McCormac, Eugene. *James K. Polk: A Political Biography.* Berkeley: University of California Press, 1922.
McGiffert, Michael. *Puritanism and the American Experience.* Reading, Mass.: Addison-Wesley, 1969.
Meyer, Donald B. *The Protestant Search for Political Realism, 1919-1941.* Berkeley: University of California Press, 1960.
Miller, Perry. *Errand into the Wilderness.* Cambridge, Mass.: Harvard University Press, 1956.
——— and Thomas H. Johnson. *The Puritans.* (See especially Vol. I, History, the Theory of the State and of Society, this World and the Next.) New York: Harper Torchbooks, 1963.
Montgomery, Bill. "Chaplain's Place? With His Troops." *Atlanta Journal-Constitution*, 7 January 1973.
Morgan, Edmund S. "Ezra Stiles and Timothy Dwight." *Proceedings of the Massachusetts Historical Society*, Vol. 72; 1963, pp. 101-117.
———. *The Puritan Dilemma: The Story of John Winthrop.* Boston: Little, Brown, 1958.
———. *Visible Saints: The History of a Puritan Idea.* New York: New York University Press, 1963.
Moskos, Charles C., Jr. "The Emergent Military: Civil, Traditional, or Plural?" *Pacific Sociological Review*, April 1973, pp. 255-280.
———. *Public Opinion and the Military Establishment.* Beverly Hills, Calif.: Sage, 1971. See especially the essay by Morris Janowitz, "The Emergent Military."
Neustadt, Richard E. *Presidential Power: The Politics of Leadership.* New York: Wiley, 1960.
Newcomb, Theodore M. *Personality and Social Change.* New York: Holt, Rinehart & Winston, 1957.
New York Times. News of the Week Section, E-5, 27 May 1973.
Nie, Norman. "Mass Belief Systems Revisited: Political Change and Attitude Structure." *Journal of Politics*, 36, 3 (August 1974), pp. 540-591.
Niebuhr, H. Richard. *Christ and Culture.* New York: Harper Torchbooks, 1956.

Bibliography

O'Connor, John J. (Chaplain, U.S.N.). *A Chaplain Looks at Vietnam.* Foreword by Senator Everett M. Dirkson. Cleveland: World, 1968.
Ozment, Steven E. *Mysticism and Dissent: Religious and Social Protest in the Sixteenth Century.* New Haven, Conn.: Yale University Press, 1973.
Pareto, Vilfredo. *The Mind and Society: A Treatise on General Sociology* (1916). Edited by Arthur Livingston, translated by Andrew Bongiorno and Arthur Livingston. New York: Dover, 1963.
Pierson, George W. *Tocqueville in America.* Garden City, N.Y.: Doubleday, 1959.
President's Committee on Religion and Welfare in the Armed Forces. *The Military Chaplaincy: A Report to the President by the President's Committee on Religion and Welfare in the Armed Forces.* Washington, D.C.: The Committee, 1950.
Preston, John. *The New Covenant, or The Saints Portion: A Treatise Unfolding the All-Sufficiencie of God, Mans Uprightness, and the Covenant of Grace.* London: "I.D.," 1630.
Roman Catholic Church. *The Official Catholic Directory, Anno Domini 1972.* New York: P. J. Kennedy, 1972.
―――. The Twenty-First Ecumenical Council of the Roman Catholic Church, 1963-1965. *The Documents of Vatican II: All Sixteen Official Texts Promulgated by the Ecumenical Council, 1963-1965, Translated from the Latin.* Edited by Walter M. Abbott and Joseph Gallager. New York: Guild Press, 1966.
Rosenau, James N. *National Leadership and Foreign Policy: A Case Study in the Mobilization of Public Support.* Princeton, N.J.: Princeton University Press, 1963.
Rousseau, Jean-Jacques. *The Social Contract and the Discourse on the Origin of Inequality* (1762 and 1755, respectively). Edited by and with an introduction by Lester Crocker. New York: Washington Square Press Pocket Books, 1967.
Russett, Bruce M. "A Countercombatant Deterrent? Feasibility, Morality, and Arms Control." Reprint from *The Military-Industrial Complex: A Reassessment,* Vol. II of the Sage Research Progress Series of War, Revolution, and Peacekeeping, Sam C. Sarkesion, Ed. Copyright 1972 by Sage Publications, Inc.
―――, and Alfred Stepan, Eds. *Military Force and American Society.* New York: Harper Torchbooks, 1973. See especially "A Personal Statement," by Major James Dickey, U.S.A., and "The New Military Professionalism," by Clarence L. Abercrombie, III, and Major Raoul H. Alcalá, U.S.A.
Sanders, Thomas G. *Catholic Innovation in a Changing Latin America.* Cuernavaca, Mexico: Centro Intercultural de Documentacion, 1969.
―――. *Protestant Concepts of Church and State: Historical Backgrounds and Approaches for the Future.* New York: Holt, Rinehart & Winston, 1964.
Sherman, Edward F. "The Civilianization of Military Law." *Maine Law Review,* Vol. 22, No. 1, 1970, pp. 3-13.
Sherrill, Robert. *Military Justice Is to Justice as Military Music Is to Music.* New York: Harper & Row, 1970.
Simon, Edith. *Luther Alive: Martin Luther and the Making of the Reformation.* Garden City, N.Y.: Doubleday, 1968.
Smith, Timothy L. *Revivalism and Social Reform in Mid-Nineteenth-Century America.* Nashville, Tenn.: Abingdon Press, 1957.

Smith, Warren T. *Thomas Coke and Early American Methodism.* Unpublished Ph.D. thesis, Boston University, 1953. Forthcoming.
Smyth, Brigadier The Rt. Hon. Sir John (VC). *In this Sign Conquer: The Story of the Army Chaplains.* London: Mowbray, 1968.
Southern Baptist Convention. *Annual of the Southern Baptist Convention, Nineteen Hundred and Seventy One.* Nashville, Tenn.: Executive Committee, Southern Baptist Convention, 1971.
Speed, B. C. "AF Chaplains Found to be Men of Great Many Roles." *Atlanta Journal,* 13 January 1973.
Stepan, Alfred. *The Military in Politics: Changing Patterns in Brazil.* Princeton, N.J.: Princeton University Press, 1971.
Stouffer, Samuel A., et al. *The American Soldier,* Vol. I, *Adjustment During Army Life.* Princeton, N.J.: Princeton University Press, 1949.
Student Rabbinic Association of the Hebrew Union College. "Report on the Chaplaincy of the Student Rabbinic Association–Jewish Institute of Religion, New York School." New York: Unpublished; xerox, 1968.
Taylor, Telford (Brigadier General, U.S.A., Ret.). *Nurmberg and Vietnam: An American Tragedy.* New York: Quadrangle, 1970.
Thayer, Carl. "Security in Viet-Nam." New Haven, Conn.: Unpublished paper for Yale University's Department of Southeast Asia Studies, 1971.
Theoharis, Athan G. *The Yalta Myths: An Issue in U.S. Politics, 1945-1955.* Columbia: University of Missouri Press, 1970.
Thibaut, John W., and Harold H. Kelley. *The Social Psychology of Groups.* New York: Wiley, 1961.
Tocqueville, Alexis de. *Democracy in America* (1835-1840). Edited by Richard D. Heffner. New York: New American Library, 1956.
Tucker, Robert W. *The Just War: A Study in Contemporary American Doctrine.* Baltimore: The Johns Hopkins University Press, 1960.
Tuveson, Ernest Lee. *Millennium and Utopia: A Study in the Background of the Idea of Progress.* Berkeley: University of California Press, 1949.
– – –. *Redeemer Nation: The Idea of America's Millennial Role.* Chicago: University of Chicago Press, 1968.
United Church of Christ. *Ministries to Military Personnel.* Philadelphia: United Church Press, 1973.
United Methodist Church. *The Book of Discipline of the United Methodist Church.* Nashville, Tenn.: Methodist Publishing House, 1968.
– – –. *General Minutes of the Annual Conferences of the United Methodist Church.* Evanston, Ill.: Section of Records and Statistics of the United Methodist Church, 1971.
– – –, Division of Interpretation, Program Council of the United Methodist Church. "What in the World is a Chaplain?" Evanston, Ill.: The Division of Interpretation, undated.
United States. *Manual for Courts-Martial, United States.* Washington, D.C.: Government Printing Office, 1969.
– – –, Department of the Army. Army Regulation 165-20. Washington, D.C.: Department of the Army, 1972.
– – –, Department of the Army. Pamphlet 165-2, "The Challenge of the Chaplaincy in the United States Army." Washington, D.C.: Department of the Army, 1970.

Bibliography

———. Field Manual 16-5, *The Chaplain*. Washington, D.C.: Department of the Army, 1964.

United States Army Chaplain School. "United States Army Active Duty Chaplain Roster." Fort Hamilton, N.Y.: U.S. Army Chaplain School, 1 January 1972.

———. "United States Army Active Duty Chaplain Roster." Fort Hamilton, N.Y.: U.S. Army Chaplain School, 1 October 1972.

Walzer, Michael. *The Revolution of the Saints: A Study in the Origins of Radical Politics.* Cambridge, Mass.: Harvard University Press, 1965.

Weber, Max. *Economy and Society: An Outline of Interpretive Sociology* (1922). Edited by Guenther Rothard Claus Wittish, translated by Ephriam Fischoff et al. New York: Bedminster Press, 1968.

———. *Max Weber on Charisma and Institution Building: Selected Papers* (1914-1924). Edited by and with an introduction by S. N. Eisenstadt. Chicago: University of Chicago Press, 1968.

———. *The Protestant Ethic and the Spirit of Capitalism* (1904-1905). Translated by Talcott Parsons. New York: Scribner, 1956.

Weltge, Ralph. "The Greening of the Military Chaplaincy." *American Report*, 4 June 1973, pp. 10-11.

Woodward, C. Vann. *The Burden of Southern History*. Baton Rouge: Louisiana State University Press, 1960.

Zahn, Gordon C. *The Military Chaplaincy: A Study of Role Tension in the Royal Air Force.* Toronto: University of Toronto Press, 1969.